DATE DUE

MAY 1 5 2017	

BRODART, CO.   Cat. No. 23-221

UNIVERSITY PRESS OF FLORIDA

- Florida A&M University, Tallahassee
- Florida Atlantic University, Boca Raton
- Florida Gulf Coast University, Ft. Myers
- Florida International University, Miami
- Florida State University, Tallahassee
- New College of Florida, Sarasota
- University of Central Florida, Orlando
- University of Florida, Gainesville
- University of North Florida, Jacksonville
- University of South Florida, Tampa
- University of West Florida, Pensacola

NATIONAL ENQUIRER

35¢

September 6, 1977   30586-2   LARGEST CIRCULATION OF ANY PAPER IN AMERICA

EXCLUSIVE...

ELVIS
THE UNTOLD STORY

Your Best Food Buys in September
page 12

★ ★ ★

1 in 3 Has a Sleep Problem That Can Shorten Life
page 8

★ ★ ★

What & How You Drink Reveals Your Personality
page 39

★ ★ ★

Govt. Officially Recognizes Ghosts
page 4

★ ★ ★

Dean Martin's New Girl: I'm Madly in Love
Page 3

★ ★ ★

How to Be a Better Listener
page 14

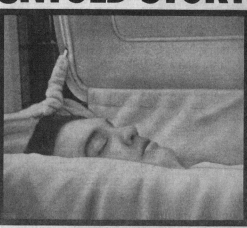

...THE LAST PICTURE

A peaceful-looking Elvis Presley lies at rest in a copper coffin in the music room of Graceland, his Memphis, Tenn., mansion. The legendary singer was dressed in a plain white suit, a blue shirt and silver tie.

6 PAGES OF EXCLUSIVE STORIES AND PHOTOS STARTING ON PAGE 20

Tabloid Valley

Supermarket News and American Culture

Paula E. Morton

University Press of Florida
Gainesville
Tallahassee
Tampa
Boca Raton
Pensacola
Orlando
Miami
Jacksonville
Ft. Myers
Sarasota

Copyright 2009 by Paula E. Morton
Printed in the United States of America. This book is
printed on Glatfelter Natures Book, a paper certified under
the standards of the Forestry Stewardship Council (FSC). It
is a recycled stock that contains 30 percent post-consumer
waste and is acid-free.

14   13   12   11   10   09   6   5   4   3   2   1

Library of Congress Cataloging-in-Publication Data
Morton, Paula E.
Tabloid Valley : supermarket news and American culture /
Paula E. Morton.
p. cm.
Includes bibliographical references and index.
ISBN 978-0-8130-3364-8 (alk. paper)
1. Tabloid newspapers—Florida—History—20th century.
2. Sensationalism in journalism—Florida—History—20th
century. I. Title.
PN4888.T3M67 2009
071.59—dc22   2008052783

The University Press of Florida is the scholarly publishing
agency for the State University System of Florida, compris-
ing Florida A&M University, Florida Atlantic University,
Florida Gulf Coast University, Florida International
University, Florida State University, New College of Florida,
University of Central Florida, University of Florida, Uni-
versity of North Florida, University of South Florida, and
University of West Florida.

University Press of Florida
15 Northwest 15th Street
Gainesville, FL 32611-2079
http://www.upf.com

For Carroll Greene,
who loved a good story

Liz Forgives Burton—He Agrees to Live With Her

65¢

NATIONAL ENQUIRER

LARGEST CIRCULATION OF ANY PAPER IN AMERICA

June 29, 1982   30586-2

How You Can Cut Cancer Risk in Half With...

VITAMINS

Horoscope Can
Guide You to a
Fantastic Summer
★ ★ ★

EXCLUSIVE

Mother of First
'Nobel' Sperm
Bank Baby Tells
Her Own Story
★ ★ ★

Women Who
Take Estrogen
Live Longer
★ ★ ★

How to Use
Makeup Like
An Expert
★ ★ ★

Meditation Can
Restore Youth

'I Killed John
Belushi'

World Exclusive—Mystery Woman Confesses

Contents

Who Mourns for the *Weekly World News?*

The best thing about subscribing to the National Enquirer *is that it arrives in the mailbox the same day as* The New York Review of Books. *How well rounded I feel.*

JOHN WATERS

People who read the tabloids deserve to be lied to.

JERRY SEINFELD

"Final Issue of
Weekly World News"
Weekly World News™
August 27, 2007.

ON SEPTEMBER 2, 2007, at three o'clock on a Sunday afternoon, more than seventy tabloid journalists and friends gathered for a wake in the Banshee Room of Brogues Irish Pub in Lake Worth, Florida. The *Weekly World News* had passed away quietly at age 28.

How better to mourn and celebrate a passing life than with an Irish wake? The deceased, a black-and-white supermarket tabloid, had been described by journalist Peter Carlson as "the most creative newspaper in American history." Its wake was an opportunity for the tabloid fraternity of writers, editors, and reporters to reminisce, drink beer, eat buffalo wings, and rock and roll to live music performed by Jody Pollard from Dublin, Ireland. "Welcome, tabloid brothers and sisters. Ain't it great to be alive and be in America!" shouted emcee and tabloid reporter Jim McCandlish. "Today we celebrate the life and times of the wackiest tabloid in the history of the world—the wild, the wonderful . . . the *Weekly World News*."

In memoriam, a photograph of the deceased, the final cover of the *Weekly World News* complete with screaming headlines, greeted the mourners at the guest registry. For a few hours the *Weekly World News*'s legendary past came to life in the back room of Brogues. Elvis serenaded half-bat, half-boy Bat Boy. A space alien in a sombrero danced with a psychic countess. "Pig-biting mad" columnist Ed Anger was caught smiling. Deceased former editor Eddie Clontz sat in spirit at the bar as a skeleton wearing a wig, hat, and a "Bat Boy Found in Cave" T-shirt. Clontz, as detailed in an obituary from the *Economist* in 2004, described himself "not as an editor but as a circus-master, drawing readers into his tent with an endless parade of fantasies and freaks."

What kind of tabloid merited obituaries in the *New York Times*, the *Washington Post* and *Time* magazine? The *Weekly World News* was not the *National Enquirer*, a publication known for unleashing a team of aggressive reporters and photographers on the O. J. Simpson murder trial to uncover a "Photo that Puts O. J. at Murder Scene." It was not the *Star*, known for its exclusive celebrity interviews, "Paris

Hilton: I'm Not a Tramp!" The iconoclastic *Weekly World News* dwelled in the most creative part of the tabloid world, from whence it gleefully reported, "Space Alien Backs Bush for President," as if the information was as newsworthy as anything covered by the mainstream media. In 1988, it boasted a circulation of over one million; in 2007 circulation barely surpassed eighty thousand. *Weekly World News* owner American Media Inc. (AMI) announced the closure was due to "challenges in the retail and wholesale magazine marketplace that have impacted the newsstand." On August 27, 2007, loyal fans and collectors of popular culture purchased the *News's* final print issue. From a benign beginning in 1979, conceived when the *National Enquirer* switched to color print and their mutual parent company's black-and-white presses sat idle, the *Weekly World News* evolved over time into an outrageous parody of tabloid sensationalism: "Siamese Twin Cuts off Brother's Head—'I Couldn't Stand His Bad Breath for One More Minute!'" "Elvis Is Alive . . . 'There Was a Double in My Coffin!'" "Abraham Lincoln Was a Woman . . . Shocking Pix Found in White House Basement!" The self-proclaimed "World's Only Reliable Newspaper" was reliably guaranteed to entertain. "Our only limit was YOUR imagination," said former editor Joe West.

Everyone at the wake wanted to know: did the demise of the *Weekly World News* signify the end of an era for a wild supermarket tabloid or its new beginning as an electronic publication at www.weekly worldnews.com? Would the *National Enquirer*, the grand dame of American tabloids, be the next to relinquish its prime real estate at the grocery store checkout counters to some glossy new celebrity magazine? What forces had the once-powerful supermarket tabloids on the ropes?

This is the story of six companion publications that have played an undeniably important role in shaping modern American media culture. Four of them—the *National Enquirer*, the *Star*, the *Globe*, and,

Chapter 1

A Small Pill, Easy to Swallow

THERE ARE NO signposts that point to Tabloid Valley. Twelve miles south of Palm Beach, Florida, a side street running through a working-class residential district of small-town Lantana abuts the sprawling one-story red brick building that once was home to the *National Enquirer* and now houses a charter school. In neighboring Lake Worth at Brogues Irish Pub, veteran tabloid reporters gather at four o'clock in the afternoon to swap stories and lift a pint or two of Guinness. Eighteen miles south of Lantana in Boca Raton, the main office of American Media Incorporated (AMI) blends indistinguishably into its corporate surroundings at the T-Rex Technology Center. The sole indication that AMI's Boca Raton office is the media headquarters of six major supermarket tabloids appears on the walls of its lobby. There, classic Page One stories live on: "Gary Hart Asked Me to Marry Him!" "Celebrity Scandals of the Year!" "An E.T. Grabbed My Laundry!"

The word "tabloid" is derived from a pharmaceutical term: a "small tablet of medicine in compressed or concentrated form," which makes it easy to swallow. In journalism, the term refers to the newspaper's reduced size, roughly half that of the *New York Times*, a traditional broadsheet newspaper. A tabloid's contents are condensed into one or two sections that open like a book, allowing it to be easily read in a café or on a subway.

"The size of the container influences the form of content and the tone. It requires a re-thinking of both news judgment, content, story forms, design and photography," said Roy Peter Clark of the Poynter Institute for Journalism. Designed to pique the curiosity of those who have not the time or inclination to read lengthy political analyses or in-depth articles, the front page resembles an eye-catching billboard and is dominated by large photographs and often sensational headlines. Because space is at a premium, the stories found on the inside of the tabloid are usually confined to one page, and the manner of writing is efficient and short. The tabloid format and style imposes strict limitations on story selection, but as in any publication, top priority is assigned to what are deemed the most important stories—a judgment which varies with the personality of the publication. On September 20, 2005, the *Washington Post* wrote, "Kerry, Edwards Criticize Bush over Response to Hurricane." On September 21, 2005, the *National Enquirer* preferred to cover "Bush's Booze Crisis!" According to anonymous "family sources," wrote the *Enquirer*, the stress resulting from the Hurricane Katrina disaster had caused President Bush to "hit the bottle again." Both publications intended to write a story that sold their product to their own group of readers.

What Sells a Tabloid Story?

Whether reported in the mainstream daily newspapers or the tabloids, a compelling story sells, but the weekly supermarket tabloids do not pretend to compete for timely hard news stories. Expect from them instead a colorful, tempting, often sensational menu of entertaining news presented as important, or else important news made entertaining.

What sort of a tabloid story sells? "A story that the reader hasn't read anywhere else, a headline that gets the reader to pick up the tabloid," said Phil Bunton, former executive editor of the *Star* and editor-in-chief of Globe Communications. A year after John F. Ken-

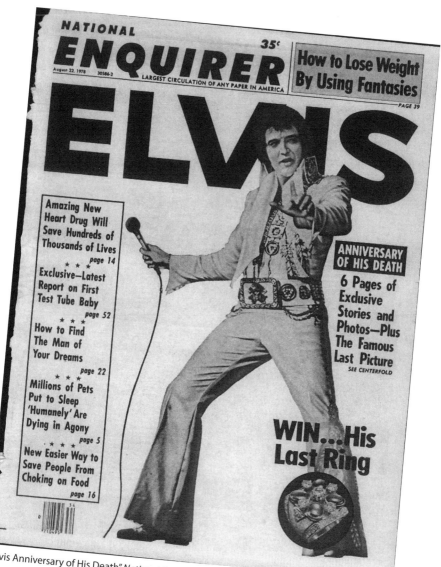

NATIONAL **ENQUIRER**

August 22, 1978   30586-2   35¢

LARGEST CIRCULATION OF ANY PAPER IN AMERICA

How to Lose Weight By Using Fantasies

PAGE 39

ELVIS

Amazing New Heart Drug Will Save Hundreds of Thousands of Lives
page 14

★ ★ ★

Exclusive—Latest Report on First Test Tube Baby
page 52

★ ★ ★

How to Find The Man of Your Dreams
page 22

★ ★ ★

Millions of Pets Put to Sleep 'Humanely' Are Dying in Agony
page 5

★ ★ ★

New Easier Way to Save People From Choking on Food
page 16

ANNIVERSARY OF HIS DEATH

6 Pages of Exclusive Stories and Photos—Plus The Famous Last Picture
SEE CENTERFOLD

WIN...His Last Ring

"Elvis Anniversary of His Death" *National Enquirer*™ August 22, 1978.

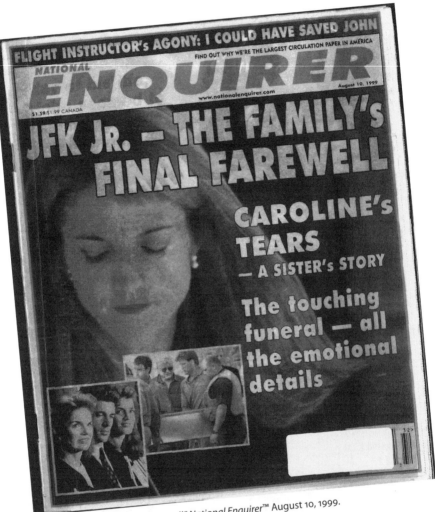

"JFK Jr.—The Family's Final Farewell" *National Enquirer*™ August 10, 1999.

nedy Jr.'s fatal plane crash, a tantalizing story continued the saga for tabloid readers, "JFK Heartbreaking Autopsy Secret, the Tragic Untold Story Never Before Revealed!" Typically, a memorable tabloid story focuses primarily on who did what, forsaking the why behind the story; for instance, "Flight Instructor's Agony: I Could Have Saved John!" Always, it appeals to the emotions, "John & Carolyn, Together Forever, Secrets They Took to the Grave." The telling photograph—"Crash Photos"—"shows the reality of the story in picture form," said Bill Bates, former photo editor for the *National Enquirer*.

The headline tells the story as unambiguously as possible, "Senator Caught with Hooker!" "You think of the headline, and then stand it up with what's known as the money quote. Without that quote, you have no story," said John Garton, former news editor of the *National Examiner*. Once the story hook is established—"He's Going to Kill Me!"—the money quote kicks in, "If I can't have you, nobody can!"

National Enquirer Memorandum

Carefully crafted quotes are tabloids' primary tool for evoking emotion. In a 1973 memorandum to his *National Enquirer* editorial staff, Generoso Pope Jr., owner and manager of the *Enquirer*, wrote, "Prod, push and probe the main characters in the story. Help them frame their answers." Pope did not ask his reporters to invent characters and events—he was honest with his readers and protected the *Enquirer* from libel—but it was up to the reporters to artfully shape the quotes that supported the story line. "Don't have the person ask for things . . . get them to tell the reader their dreams and their hopes," he told his reporters. "Don't say, 'We're broke and we need money to buy a house in a better neighborhood.' Say, 'My dream is that someday we'll be able to get out of this rat hole and give Ricky a clean, warm bed . . . he's never asked for much . . . he deserves to die with a little dignity.'"

A Tabloid Story

The first priority of a tabloid story is to amuse, amaze, or shock—often it is a story no one else wants or dares to pursue. In 1975 a single-column story describing Secretary of State Kissinger's garbage appeared on an inside page in the *National Enquirer*. It was not an exposé about actor Rock Hudson's romantic life, nor was it a revelation about the health benefits of wine. In fact, it "probably would not have made the paper at all had the gathering of it not been a worldwide sensation," said the reporter on the story, Jay Gourley.

Generoso Pope Jr., the owner and hands-on manager of the *Enquirer*, was curious; what might Henry Kissinger's garbage reveal? At midnight on the eighth of July, Gourley confiscated five garbage bags outside Kissinger's Georgetown, D.C., home. He managed to throw the bags into the trunk of his car and lock it before Secret Service agents and city police arrived and detained him outside Kissinger's home for over three hours while they debated if the garbage bags, left on the curb, were public or private property. Although the police submitted a report, Gourley was not arrested.

Admittedly, the contents of the garbage bags did not contain highly classified documents, but they did include privileged and personal information: Secret Service agents' work assignments, old travel plans, a report regarding the loss of a firearm by a Secret Service agent, discarded dinner invitations, pharmacy envelopes, and shopping lists.

A partial list of the contents, especially the personal items, vaguely interested the *Enquirer* readers, but far more important to Kissinger and mainstream journalism was the method the *Enquirer* employed to obtain the story. Was the trash placed on the curb considered public domain? Was the acquisition an invasion of privacy? Was the *Enquirer*'s mission clever news-gathering or deceitful and distasteful? "It was an important story," said Gourley, "because it attracted national and international interest and reflected a divide in the camp; those who admired the *National Enquirer* and said the *National Enquirer* did a good job, went the extra mile to get a story and accurate information. The critics said it was garbage journalism and an invasion of privacy. The incident was a confirmation of the two conflicting opinions."

Undeterred by the controversy, Pope created a follow-up story. He invited the mainstream media to photograph Gourley as he returned the garbage bags to the curb. If Kissinger was so upset, Pope said, the *Enquirer* would give him back his trash.

A week later a reporter from the *Palm Beach Post* raided the garbage bin in the back of the *Enquirer's* offices in Lantana and retrieved an outdated memorandum from Pope instructing his reporters to ask leading questions. This was hardly the scandalous discovery they had likely hoped for, as it was and still is a technique often employed by many media sources.

These controversial news-gathering methods set the supermarket tabloids apart from mainstream journalism. The "tabs" pay for information and exclusives. Checkbook journalism encourages an anonymous source to disclose that broadcaster Rush Limbaugh was suspected of abusing narcotics. Cash buys the incriminating photograph of Senator Gary Hart vacationing with a woman other than his wife. It locks up Gennifer Flowers's exclusive story of her provocative relationship with a future president of the United States.

Are the stories true? "We didn't have to make it up. It was there for the taking," said former *Star* editor Joanna Elm. An astute tabloid journalist recognizes the nucleus of a tabloid story in a two- or three-paragraph news item or a celebrity rumor, and transforms it into the untold story, tabloid style.

Is the information accurate? "The general danger is that if you pay people for information it is going to be more suspect, less likely to be truthful—more hype, not false necessarily, but hype," said Jack Doppelt, journalism professor at Northwestern University. Yet Da-

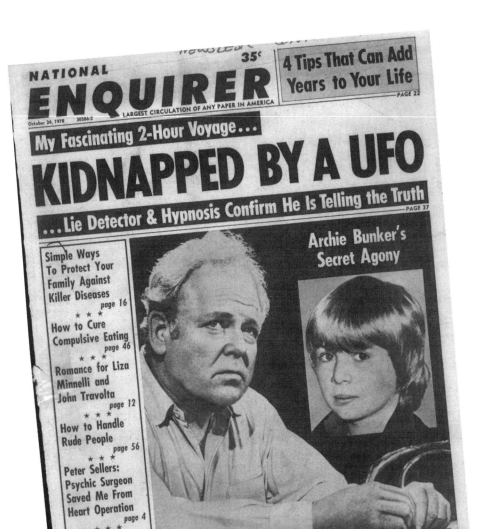

NATIONAL **ENQUIRER**

35¢

LARGEST CIRCULATION OF ANY PAPER IN AMERICA

October 24, 1978   30586-2

4 Tips That Can Add Years to Your Life
PAGE 22

My Fascinating 2-Hour Voyage...

KIDNAPPED BY A UFO

...Lie Detector & Hypnosis Confirm He Is Telling the Truth
PAGE 37

Simple Ways To Protect Your Family Against Killer Diseases
page 16

★ ★ ★

How to Cure Compulsive Eating
page 46

★ ★ ★

Romance for Liza Minnelli and John Travolta
page 12

★ ★ ★

How to Handle Rude People
page 56

★ ★ ★

Peter Sellers: Psychic Surgeon Saved Me From Heart Operation
page 4

★ ★ ★

How to Cope With Bad Days
page 14

Archie Bunker's Secret Agony

Carroll O'Connor's Son, 16, Fights Cancer

While "All in the Family" fans laugh, Carroll O'Connor has been crying on the inside. And his heartbreak has taken a terrible toll on his health as he's watched his son (inset) battle a deadly cancer. "He adores our son Hugh, and he's been in agony seeing him go through all this," reveals O'Connor's wife in an exclusive interview. (P. 28.)

"Kidnapped by a UFO" *National Enquirer*™ October 24, 1978.

vid Perel, editor-in-chief of the *National Enquirer*, said, "Checkbook journalism is a tool, powerful and effective if used correctly." Whether the information for a story idea is bought or gratis, the facts and the sources must be verified.

Is the source credible? All journalism places responsibility on sources for credible information and experts to back up that information. Most of the sources enlisted by the tabloid reporters are trusted confidential contacts, usually anonymous to the readers. In covering a political scandal or a medical breakthrough, the viability of the tabloid's fact-based story depends on credible sources. When discussing a gossipy innuendo or a psychic prediction, the nature of the subject invites skepticism.

Does paying for information give a reporter the edge? "It depends on the coverage," said Steven Edwards, United Nations correspondent and former *Star* reporter. "It has long been common practice when covering the celebrity world, especially to entice people who have access to the stars, but who likely don't have a great deal of money, like a housekeeper or limo driver. But in heavy political coverage, the emphasis is to appeal to people's honor, and offering money would be considered crass, even corrupt."

A story built around a celebrity rumor or scandal is vetted for libel by fact-checkers and tabloid attorneys. In 1976, as a result of actor Carol Burnett's successful defamation suit against the *National Enquirer*, Generoso Pope Jr. hired Ruth Annan, previously with *Time* magazine, to direct the research department. "We police the copy," she said. "We verify the quotes that are in the stories, the background information." On the other hand, anthropologist S. Elizabeth Bird argued, "One problem of course is that, even if every quote included may be 'accurate,' the research department can only confirm that this 'fact' was said by someone."

The Fact-Checkers

In 1923 *Time* magazine pioneered a strict fact-checking system that Generoso Pope Jr. adopted in 1976 as his first line of defense against libel suits. The *National Enquirer* research department required the writers and reporters to submit their transcripts for meticulous scrutiny. Mostly women, four or five fact-checkers brought hardened reporters to their knees. Savvy reporters learned to tape the entire interview, write the story with quotes, and then phone and read it to the person interviewed, once again on tape. "After reading back hair-raising, colorful, first-person accounts of shark attacks to people who were monosyllabic, they'd invariably say: 'That's incredible. How did you know all that? That's exactly what was going through my mind,'" said reporter Jim McCandlish. The taped interview and the read-back required extra time and work, but it usually meant acceptance by the fact-checkers.

The Tabloid Photographer

The tabloid photographer, armed with cameras, extreme close-up zoom lenses, tape recorder, binoculars, and cash, is as bold and quick-thinking as the tabloid reporter. Backed by ample financial resources, the *National Enquirer* initially kept photographers on staff, but recently, the tabloids have transitioned to hiring out professional freelance photographers who either contract with a photo editor for a specific assignment or independently shoot photographs that are sold on the open market to the highest bidder.

"There were no such things as a 40-hour week for tabloid photographers," said Jim Leggett, a photojournalist who worked for three of the Florida supermarket tabloids. "Holidays, family celebrations, anniversaries were missed when the phone rang, *Star* photo editor

"Brad & Angelina Caught Together" *Star*™ May 9, 2005.

Alistair Duncan on the line asking, 'Jim, can you do a wee job for me?'" Exclusive stories are guarded with secrecy, sometimes from the photographers themselves. Even Leggett, as the *Enquirer* senior photo editor, was not always informed about the details of a sensitive assignment. He was handed a lead sheet with the story number, editor's signature, and "SECRET" marked in place of the story name and angle.

Frequently, the celebrity tabloids all receive an identical tip. In October 1988, former Reuters reporter Mike McDonough and photographer Jim Leggett, both fired from the *Enquirer* and working for the competing *Star*, were sent to the Caribbean island of Curacao, Venezuela, to track down honeymooners Lisa Marie Presley, the daughter of Elvis Presley, and musician Danny Keough. The newlywed couple was discovered aboard a Scientology cruise ship, preparing to depart that evening. McDonough spotted one of the *Enquirer*'s senior reporters on the ship's deck. "Finding ourselves in serious danger of being scooped, we quickly came to a rather diabolic decision," said Leggett. "If we couldn't get aboard, he was getting off." Leggett demanded to see the captain and announced, "We'd very much like to do a story on your Scientology cruise." Predictably, the captain replied, "No tabloid reporters allowed." The *Star* team nodded in the direction of the stowaway reporter and informed the captain, "He's from the *Enquirer*." Furious, their former colleague was hustled off the ship. "Bastards!" he howled, "I'm gonna kill you!"

Tabloid Valley Roots

Unquestionably, Generoso Pope Jr. forged a new path when he brought the tabloid culture to the American supermarkets. "But although tabloids really made their mark on American culture in the 1980s, they were hardly new," said anthropologist S. Elizabeth Bird. She suggested that the cultural roots of the American tabloids trace back to seventeenth-century folk narrative delivered in ballads and upon newssheets. In the nineteenth century, innovations by Ameri-

The Paparazzi

"Paparazzi" is a pejorative term for aggressive celebrity-stalking photographers, popularized by Paparazzo, a character starring in Italian director Federico Fellini's film, "La Dolce Vita." In one Italian dialect, "paparazzo" refers to a loud, buzzing, pesky mosquito.

Celebrity news sells tabloids and the celebrity photograph—a candid shot of a private moment, frequently without consent, or a posed opportunity at a red-carpet event—sells the story. Is the tabloid photographer intrusive or is the celebrity's loss of privacy the price of fame? In America, the First Amendment protects the right to freedom of the press, and, in fact, high-profile publicity can be a boon for celebrities. However, particularly since the 1997 fatal accident of paparazzi-pursued Princess Diana and Dodi Fayed, tabloid photographers are associated with the "paparazzi." Photojournalist Jim Leggett said, "While we [tabloid photographers] chased down reclusive celebrities, crooked politicians or people making news, I never ran with, nor considered myself, paparazzi." In his pursuit of celebrity photographs he said,

My first try was to obtain permission to shoot via an agent, family member or friend. If that failed, I would find a local contact, hoping to discover where and when I might find the quarry. Sometimes this would lead to an invitation from the subject—once they became aware I was trying for pictures. As a last resort I would stake them out—more often contacting some local photographer to do so. To acquire a photograph I was never confrontational, pushy or demanding, trusting more on congenial chat and gentle persuasion. Of course, I'd point out if the subject gave me permission, they would avoid being beset by an avalanche of lesser photographers.

can penny newspapers revived the tradition of amusing, titillating, and shocking readers with entertaining stories. To make the human interest story realistic, reporters canvassed the streets, employing a reporting technique called "leg-work," which was developed out of necessity by James Gordon Bennett in 1836 and later embraced by the supermarket tabloids. When a piece of printing machinery broke, Bennett's *New York Herald* was unable to publish what would have likely been a sellout issue covering the axe murder of Helen Jewett, a beautiful prostitute. When the presses were repaired two days later, Bennett and his team of reporters wrote stories of intrigue and speculation about "The Recent Tragedy." They viewed the mutilated body in the bedroom of Madame Rosina Townsend's high-class brothel, interviewed neighbors, fellow prostitutes, and police investigators, and ultimately uncovered a witness who claimed an elegant man in a black cloak slipped out of Jewett's room on the night of the murder. Of course, editorialized Bennett, the mysterious man could have been one of the wealthy and powerful brothel customers carefully shielded from suspicion or exposure and contributing to the moral depravity of the city.

Yellow Journalism

The penny papers of the nineteenth century were more interesting to read than dry financial reports and political party news, but their physical appearance remained stodgy. The importance of visual appeal was not fully appreciated by American newspapers until the late 1800s when publishing magnates Joseph Pulitzer and William Randolph Hearst revolutionized the front page with vividly drawn illustrations, colored newsprint, and bold banner headlines calculated by Hearst to "bite like a bullet."

Joseph Pulitzer and William Randolph Hearst were the major practicers of "Yellow Journalism," a technique that matched aggressive reporting with dramatic storytelling and vivid descriptions using conversational language. In 1883 Joseph Pulitzer introduced the *New York World*, "a paper made for the million, for the masses," filled with news that "is original, distinctive, dramatic, romantic, thrilling, unique, curious, quaint, humorous, odd, apt to be talked about." In 1896, when William Randolph Hearst bought the *New York Journal*, he emulated Pulitzer's style and added the gee-whiz story—a story that was so amazing that, indeed, the reader would say, "gee-whiz" (a style of journalism which would later become a Generoso Pope Jr. favorite). Although Pulitzer's and Hearst's editorial mix—political scandals, tenement murders, society gossip, popular advice columns, and romance stories especially directed towards a female audience—was a big step toward the supermarket tabloid formula, the format remained a broadsheet newspaper, not the handy tabloid.

As Pulitzer and Hearst engaged in a circulation war, the stakes for readership escalated. The two publishers vied for the most sensational impact, leading to accusations of exaggerating and manipulating the truth, a complaint that has frequently been made of the supermarket tabloids. In 1897 Hearst assigned the famous illustrator Frederic Remington to raise the profile of the Cuban revolt against the Spaniards. After a reluctant President William McKinley yielded to public opinion and declared war on Spain, Hearst bragged, "How Do You Like Our War?"

Photo Power

With the advent of camera technology in the twentieth century, the photojournalist supplanted the sketch artist. By the 1920s technology had improved the 35mm still camera to include flash powder, which was succeeded by the flash bulb. An incriminating photograph was exactly what a jazzy tabloid in the Roaring '20s required to feed a scandal.

The power of photographs confirmed the value of the tabloid form of journalism in America. The most outrageous and short-lived of

New York City's picture tabloids was the *New York Graphic*, published in 1924 by physical fitness advocate Bernarr Macfadden. Macfadden advocated walking several miles a day, taking vitamins, and, of course, reading his sex- and crime-filled tabloid.

The *Graphic*, labeled the "Porno-Graphic" by its detractors, pushed the limits of sensationalism by playing up scandals with fabricated pictures, usually with sexual connotations. Retouchers cut and pasted separate photographs to create photographic collages called "composographs." Basically, they put people where they were not: Place "A" (celebrity face) on "B" (naked model of a newsroom copyboy) at "C" (the boudoir of a famous actor). While the future *Weekly World News* would amuse with a composite of former first lady Hillary Clinton holding an adopted alien baby, the *Graphic* offended with lewd bedroom scenes of millionaire Edward "Daddy" Browning and his child bride, Peaches. Advertisers boycotted and libel suits proliferated.

"The Composite Gallery"

A glance through the "Composite Gallery" in Frank Mallen's *Sauce for the Gander* illustrates the complexity and outrageousness of the *New York Graphic*'s composites. It took twenty separate photographs and a model willing to strip to the waist for the courtroom scene of the "Rhinelander Bride" divorce. A composite of twenty-five photographs detailed Earl Carroll's wild bathtub party for his high-society friends. Gathered around a well-known female actor, naked in a bathtub, was a group of equally well-known gentlemen in tuxedos. Ten photographs produced the hospital scene depicting an ailing Rudolph Valentino on the operating table, a nurse stroking his head while the doctor raises a scalpel. After the actual operation failed and Valentino died, a psychic claimed she had contacted Rudolph Valentino's spirit. Inspired, the *Graphic* orchestrated Valentino's afterlife, "Valentino Is in Heaven with Enrico Caruso: Rudy Meets Caruso, Tenor's Spirit Speaks!"

After only eight years the *New York Graphic* faded out of the cosmographic picture into tabloid history, but the *New York Daily News*, "New York's Picture Newspaper," has survived since 1919 as a daily city tabloid covering local and national news. From its inception, the *Daily News* recognized the photograph as a powerful way to convey information and evoke emotion.

In 1928 a single bold headline and photograph mesmerized the readers of the *Daily News*. Below the headline, "Dead!" sat the limp body of Ruth Snyder, convicted of murdering her husband, strapped in an electric chair. Without the photograph, the written version of the execution could have been adjusted to allay the morbidity of the affair. The image of a woman just electrocuted, however, obtained by a photographer posing as a witness, left nothing to the imagination. Protestors cited the photograph as an example of the tabloid's poor taste; supporters claimed the public had the right to know—and see. Encouraged by the sale of more than one million copies on the first day alone, the *Daily News* reprinted subsequent editions, which also sold out.

Eager to be part of the excitement of the picture tabloids, William Randolph Hearst returned in 1924 to the New York City publishing scene with the *New York Daily Mirror*, heralded as "New York's Best Picture Newspaper." The "*Daily Mirror*'s program will be 90 per cent entertainment, 10 per cent information—and the information without boring you," Hearst announced. A lavish amount of photographs illustrated short, sensational news stories, Walter Winchell wrote a popular gossip column, and young writers such as Ring Lardner Jr. contributed entertaining human interest stories. After running for over forty years, the *Daily Mirror* folded in 1972.

On the sidelines of the New York City tabloid community, William Griffin, a colleague of Hearst who was once employed as a compositor by the *Graphic*, published the Sunday *New York Enquirer*, founded in 1926. Its stories were poorly written and their veracity questionable. On Sunday morning, December 7, 1941, shortly after 11 a.m. eastern standard time, Japanese warplanes bombed Pearl Harbor. The *New York Enquirer* stopped the presses so that their paper was the first in New York City to publish the momentous news. Unfortunately for Griffin, most of the paper's reader base had eroded and the scoop was barely acknowledged.

In 1952 Griffin was looking for a buyer for the *New York Enquirer* and Generoso Pope Jr. was looking for a business. Pope referred to his new purchase as "a dumping ground for publicity agents and columnists who wrote for free and couldn't get their stuff printed anywhere else." In a *New York Times* interview he said he intended to change the *New York Enquirer* into a national weekly that focused on stories derived from serious events, shifting away from personality-driven pieces. "It would not," Pope declared, "become a tabloid."

Chapter 2

The Man and His Vision

"IN AN AGE darkened by the menace of totalitarian tyranny and war the *New York Enquirer* will fight for the rights of man—the rights of the individual, and will champion human decency and dignity, freedom and peace." In 1952, when the United States was embroiled in the Korean War as well as the cold war, a patriotic Generoso Pope Jr. envisioned a noble mission for his Sunday *New York Enquirer*. That same year, Robert Harrison, alumnus of the *New York Graphic*, founded *Confidential*, a Hollywood gossip and scandal magazine that in the opinion of *Time* was "based on the proposition that millions like to wallow in scurrility." Libel suits and their ensuing financial settlements increased at a faster rate than the *Confidential*'s sales and eventually led to the magazine's demise, but not before Pope noted its large readership of over 4 million. The *New York Enquirer* was fortunate if its circulation reached 75,000.

When Pope purchased the *New York Enquirer* he acquired a ten cents-a-copy almost bankrupt mixture of "Horses to Watch," a "TV Selecter," "The Racy Memoirs of Miss Pat Ward," and poorly written stories manufactured from police reports and rumors. For his first issue, released on April 7, 1952, Pope produced an exclusive of timely national significance; General Matthew B. Ridgeway had been selected to replace General Dwight D. Eisenhower as commander in chief of the Allied forces in Europe. Horseracing fans skipped to the racing odds in the back pages, and journalists at the global newswire dismissed the news as one more incident of a concocted story by the *New York Enquirer.*

Pope was cash poor, an underdog in the crowded urban newspaper market, and his editorial choices had bombed. Piles of unsold issues exposing defense contract abuses or state tax schemes were replaced each Sunday afternoon with new editions that succumbed to the same fate. It was an uncomfortable situation, but hardly an insurmountable challenge for the son of a successful and determined entrepreneur who built a business and fortune from the ground up.

Generoso Pope Jr., the third son, was raised in a wealthy and powerful household, visited by politicians, judges, police commissioners, and prominent members of the Italian community. In 1906 Pope's father, surname Papa, sailed from Sicily to New York City on the ocean liner *Madonna.* Generoso Sr. came to the United States to make his fortune. With patience, hard work, and a sharp business mind, he achieved his goal. Papa changed his name to Pope and shoveled sand and drove a cement truck for a company he eventually bought, Colonial Sand and Cement. It would become one of the largest cement companies in the New York City metro area. Pope Sr. paved his way to wealth by building roads and constructing the foundations of New York City landmarks such as the Radio City Music Hall and Rockefeller Center. He expanded his influence when he bought *Il Progresso,* the largest North American Italian-language newspaper.

Pope Sr. groomed his third son to lead *Il Progresso.* At age fifteen Pope Jr. was paying the newspaper's bills. At age nineteen, after graduating with an engineering degree from the Massachusetts Institute of Technology, he was named editor.

When Pope Sr. suddenly died of a heart attack, Pope Jr. was left without his father as an advocate in a family whose ambitions and emotions ran high. He was plunged to the bottom of the family hierarchy, taking orders from his mother and older brothers, and he was removed from his position as editor of *Il Progresso*. Not surprisingly, he severed ties with his family and forged his own path.

Diverted from his prescribed career as publisher, Pope Jr. joined the Central Intelligence Agency, where he spent his time confined to an office, writing propaganda for the Psychological Warfare Unit. He lasted not quite a year. "I really got fed up with government bureaucracy. You'd spend weeks trying to get things done and then you couldn't do it," Pope commented in an interview with journalist William Amlong.

What Pope could do was run a newspaper. When he learned that the *New York Enquirer* was for sale for seventy-five thousand dollars, he borrowed money toward the purchase price, presumably from his baptismal godfather "Uncle Frank" Costello, an alleged racketeer boss. Regardless of life-long innuendos of his connections with Cos-

Circulation Sales

The *New York Enquirer*, like its supermarket tabloid successors, depended more on weekly circulation sales at the news outlets than on subscription sales. Circulation sales are considered more profitable because the single-copy price is higher than the discounted subscription price, but while the subscription sale is guaranteed, the circulation sale is an impulse buy. Making circulation sales requires a shrewd calculation of what the consumer wants to read and what makes a given publication stand out from the competition. Generoso Pope Jr. was constantly evaluating the circulation value of the *New York Enquirer*. When it evolved into the *National Enquirer*, Pope gambled that greater circulation sales generated by the high visibility of a conspicuous and entertaining tabloid at the supermarket checkout counters would yield more profit than advertising revenue and subscription sales would. He won.

tello, Pope succeeded through his own wits and determination. Gifted with the same tenacity, work ethic, and intelligence that had catapulted his father to prosperity and power, Pope built a business. He was twenty-five years old.

What would distinguish, at a quick first glance, the *New York Enquirer* from the other newspapers at the corner newsstand? What would entice a busy New Yorker to stop and buy his paper? Pope experimented with different appearances and themes until he found an approach that worked, and when the public tired of it, he once more adjusted it. During the next ten years he took the skeleton of a tabloid and fleshed it out with innovations that eventually produced the most widely read weekly tabloid in North America.

Initially, Pope changed the format from a broadsheet eight-column newspaper to a compact tabloid. Requiring less paper to print, the move was wise economically, and additionally proved popular with urban readers. One letter to the editor read, "I am very pleased with the new *Enquirer* and hope you will continue it in tabloid form. The print is easier on the eyes, the paper is smaller in size but larger in content and it is much easier to read, regardless of whether one is traveling or just relaxing in a chair."

Once Pope simplified the page format to the tabloid, he turned his attention to the content. He concluded that if the best-selling New York City tabloids offered sensational fare, then he would have to abandon his personal crusades to give the readers what they wanted, "Torture Cult Sex Orgies Bared Here." In the guise of public service, "Teensters Wallow in Liquor and Sex" warned parents of their children's misdeeds. "Serves Tea in Bed, Then the Ax" suggested the dark humor of a headline editor. Inside pages offered seven celebrity gossip columns but celebrities did not rate a feature story. The reliable standby was the Hialeah Park horse-racing forms.

The *New York Enquirer* as a tabloid attracted readers but hardly improved its reputation among those expecting hard news. A reader wrote to the editor, "I read the rag you call a newspaper and in my opinion it is a filthy rag. All the news you have is about sex, dope and smut. Here is the paper I bought, please return my dime." The New York City Board of Higher Education agreed. Mayor Wagner announced that the tone and content of the *New York Enquirer* were not appropriate for Pope's board appointment. Too preoccupied with survival to dwell on the affront, Pope resigned. He put community service and philanthropy on pause until he was flush with success in Tabloid Valley.

As the shock value of the *New York Enquirer* rose, so did Pope's profits, but once tabloids were recognized as a profitable enterprise, competitors flooded the market. Circulation sales reached a plateau, a situation unacceptable to a true entrepreneur. Pope needed to capture the attention that would propel the *New York Enquirer* above the competition. The idea came to him at the scene of an automobile accident, about which lay strewn twisted metal, bloody bodies, and injured victims screaming in pain. Before Pope rushed past the accident—he hated the sight of blood—he observed how people stopped and stared. They were transfixed by the morbid scene of carnage. "I noticed how auto accidents drew crowds, and I decided if it was blood that interested people, I'd give it to them," explained Pope. The *New York Enquirer* entered the phase that became known as its gore years.

Pope hired a hardy staff of reporters and photographers that choked down their revulsion and dutifully rushed to the gruesome scenes of terrible accidents and particularly gory murders. Pope's tabloid contained no offensive sex but was replete with bloody gore described and photographed in lurid detail. "It bothered the hell out of me running that kind of a paper, but it was paying the bills and, after all those lean years, it was a good feeling to have some money in the bank," admitted Pope. By the mid-1950s, Pope had attained sufficient financial leverage to expand the *New York Enquirer* into the *National Enquirer*, initially distributed to the tri-state area of New York, New Jersey, and Connecticut, and then throughout America.

"The Duchess" Virginia Marmaduke

"That's the way, kid! You got a big scoop there. Now, just like the old days in Chicago," said "The Duchess" Virginia Marmaduke to her nephew Larry Haley when he broke an important story for the *National Enquirer*. Virginia Marmaduke was a pioneer female crime reporter, and to her the old days were the 1940s and '50s, before the overwhelming power of television and the Internet took hold, when people still listened to the radio and read newspapers for news and entertainment. Nicknamed "The Duchess" by an editor who wanted an easy name to shout, she covered "blood, guts and sex—not necessarily in that order" for the *Chicago Sun* and the *Chicago Tribune*. She was exactly Generoso Pope Jr.'s style of reporter. On a stakeout, she attacked a mobster with her spike-heeled shoe. She was the only newspaper reporter at the fresh crime scene of 6-year-old Suzanne Degnan, who had been decapitated and dumped in a city sewer. Upon Virginia Marmaduke's death at age ninety-three, her friends at her alma mater, Southern Illinois University, recalled her passion for journalism. "'Remember,' she'd say, laughing her throaty hah-hah-hah, 'newspapering won't make you into a millionaire, but it sure helps you live a full life.'"

How Gory was the Gore?

How gory was the gore? As gory as, "I Cut Out Her Heart and Stomped on It!" On April 6, 1963, in Reno, Nevada, Sonja McCaskie, a beautiful young Olympic alpine skier from Scotland, was brutally murdered and dismembered. The *Washington Post* ran nine short paragraphs, with no accompanying photographs, under the headline, "Dismembered Body of Girl Skier Found." The tone was factual. The *Nevada State Journal* framed the "butcher killing" with two photographs of an empty bloodied hope chest and a yearbook photo of the victim under the headline, "Police Hunt Clues in Butcher Killing." The tone was sober and frightening. The *National Enquirer* filed the news clippings under "murders" and waited nearly five months to produce its exclusive, "I Cut Out Her Heart and Stomped on It!" The tone was, of course, sensational.

Timeliness was of little importance to the *Enquirer* as long as it produced an exclusive. It would have preferred the gruesome photographs from the crime scene that recalled a butcher shop littered with carnage, including a torso stuffed in a cedar hope chest, a severed foot wrapped in a bloody blanket, and a heart on the living room floor, but official photographs were not released. The *Enquirer* put out the word that they would give cash for photos, and predictably, a local resident, who reportedly raided the autopsy photographs from the morgue, supplied the *Enquirer* with the components for a story that satisfied their readers. Horror was reading about the murder; gore was seeing the torso of a decapitated body, a dismembered foot, the right one if you read the gruesome details, and an extracted heart.

Not all the content of the *Enquirer* was blood and violence. A drug to cure swearing, a mathematical child wonder, a four-ton hippopotamus, and a bald woman whose hair fell out after using dye on it amazed nearly one hundred thousand readers a week. "Usually the formula for the full page center spread was one photograph of a cute baby, one 'cheesecake' model, one celebrity and one gory accident scene," said Barney Giambalvo, former production manager. "Unless the gore picture was extra sensational—then gore covered the page." One of Giambalvo's most memorable recollections of his first week at the *Enquirer* is a full page center spread that pictured the body of a man who had been run over by seventy-five train cars. The photograph of the victim, retouched to clearly show his exposed brains, eminently qualified for the solo position and prompted several newsstands to display the center spread instead of the cover to lure customers.

To accommodate the demand for a constant supply of stories, Pope liberally used a nationwide network of freelancers, called stringers, who wrote a story based on a news event and sent it to the home office to be rewritten, tabloid style. The *Enquirer's* London Bureau coordinated a European network of international reporters and photojournalists who in contrast submitted a tabloid story ready to print with quotes and photographs that matched the headline. In a few years Pope would capitalize on the expertise of the British to lead the *Enquirer* to the supermarkets.

A Celebrity Story

By 1960 the *National Enquirer* was capturing its share of readers who craved gore and gee-whiz stories, but Pope wanted to find out what interested the rest of the potential tabloid readership. Photo editor Bill Bates, conditioned at United Press International to think in terms of personality feature stories based on news events, suggested a story about Clark Gable's wife and baby. Four months after actor Clark Gable, the "King of Hollywood," died of a heart attack on November 16, 1960, his son was born. So what happened to his wife and newborn son?

The *Enquirer*, known for graphic images of destruction, was not a likely candidate for a celebrity lifestyle interview. Pope asked, "How do we get the pix and interviews?" "No problem," Bates said. Pope was off and running, "Can you get on it, right away?"

Ted Munch, as executive editor, coordinated a network of contacts, freelance reporters, and photographers to produce a Hollywood celebrity story. In addition to readers of gory mishaps and crimes, the *Enquirer* now reached out to readers of gossip. By the end of the decade, a wide variety of stories ranging from medical cures to celebrity news became the mainstay of the *Enquirer*.

The Competition

The *National Enquirer* was eagerly read, boycotted, or imitated. Despite the gore, Pope avoided official censorship; the *Enquirer* exploited violence, not sex. Across the border in Montreal, Canada, explicit sexual matter in the print media proliferated until Montreal instituted a new policy. As soon as sex-filled tabloids were delivered to the newsstands, the police removed them. John Vader, editor of the racy Montreal-based *Midnight*, turned to the successful *Enquirer* for inspiration and traveled to the New York City Public Library to study back issues. Since Vader and his partner, Joe Azaria, did not possess Pope's financial resources and were thus unable to sustain a flow of fresh weekly tabloid stories and photographs, they improvised by recycling previously published crime and accident stories from the *Enquirer*. Soon a revised version of *Midnight* appeared on the newsstands in the United States and survived to become one of the Tabloid Valley weeklies, renamed the *Globe*.

Nationally, *Midnight* and three Chicago-based tabloids, the *National Insider*, *National Tattler*, and *National Informer* shared the newsstand with the *Enquirer*. Although they vied for dominance with competing sensationalism, they were unable to overtake Pope's loyal customer base or obtain such a strong financial cushion and as many national distribution contacts.

Distribution Is the Key

When Generoso Pope Jr. converted the *New York Enquirer* into a national publication he realized the value of a large and visible marketplace presence. Certainly, the content and packaging of an eye-catching front page were important, but the critical component was distribution. Initially, Pope established influential contacts with many of the national newsstands, the primary sales outlet for the *National Enquirer*. By the end of the 1960s he adapted the *Enquirer* for supermarket sales and created Distribution Services Inc. (DSI), thereby taking control of 65 percent of the supermarket magazine sales racks. DSI became the *Enquirer*'s distribution system to ensure maximum exposure at the checkout counter. It was a moneymaker for Pope.

Far ahead of the competition, the *National Enquirer* prospered until circulation sales for all the weekly tabloids leveled off at newsstands. Pope trusted his instinct for editorial direction, but he reviewed economic reports and population shifts for marketing advice. In the 1960s the movement from the city to the suburbs produced a dramatic effect upon lifestyle habits and consumer spending. The all-inclusive supermarket supplanted the corner green grocer, butcher shop, and especially pertinent to tabloid sales, the newsstand. Television and the introduction of home video created a new market for celebrities, and television star Lucille Ball was as popular as movie actor Warren Beatty. Furthermore, with time at a premium, commuters preferred the short and entertaining stories in *Readers Digest*, which was available at the supermarkets.

New Image, New Market

In order to grow, the *Enquirer* needed a different image and a different market. "We had saturated the gore market, and since this is a business, I knew we had to change," Pope said in a 1972 interview, aptly titled "*Enquirer*: Violence Gets the Ax." In Great Britain, Rupert Murdoch's Sunday tabloid, *News of the World*, sold more than 6 million copies a week. "If *News of the World* can sell that many papers in Britain, we should be able to sell at least three times as many in this country," Pope said.

Who and where were such a large group of consumers? They were women shopping in suburban supermarkets who did not want to bring home the *Enquirer* with a decapitated body pictured on its cover. The *Enquirer* was a sleazy tabloid known as "that gory one," with cheap newsprint that rubbed off on one's fingertips. It published horror stories about incidents of cockroaches scurrying under packages of meat and a mouse corpse found in a pickle jar at the very supermarkets Pope needed as his allies. But Pope was an entrepreneur who believed in acting on an opportunity and taking a calculated risk for a profitable outcome. He proved to be a "genius at anticipating what the reader wanted before the reader knew it," said reporter Jim McCandlish.

"I'm envisioning a *Readers Digest* in tabloid form," Pope announced. "Roasted Corpse of Baby Found in an Incinerator" was replaced with "U.S. Ranks 25th in Male Life Expectancy; 14th in Female . . . a Shocking Indictment of the American Medical System." Reportedly, Joseph Sorrentino, Allied News publisher of the Chicago tabloids, expressed the sentiments of the loyal readers of gore, "What's dis guy think he's doin'? Has he gone nuts or somethin? Where's all da chopped-up bodies?"

"Pope did what no one else had done," said former associate editor Malcolm Balfour. He transformed the *Enquirer* from a gory tabloid into a uniquely American one suitable for suburban supermarkets

NATIONAL

ENQUIRER

30¢

EXTRA—22 Special Christmas Features

LARGEST CIRCULATION OF ANY PAPER IN AMERICA

December 23, 1975

Top U.S. Cancer Research Team Reports...

BREAST CANCER TREATMENT —BIGGEST BREAKTHROUGH EVER

—PAGE 4

Exclusive Interview
With Ted Kennedy:
The Heartaches &
Joys of Raising 16
Kennedy Children
page 3

★ ★ ★

How Christmas
Cards Reveal
Personality
page 13

★ ★ ★

Police Woman's
Earl Holliman:
How the Censors
Cramp Our Style
page 35

★ ★ ★

5 Tips to Help You
Wake Up Alert
page 28

★ ★ ★

A Christmas
Message by
Billy Graham
page 6

★ ★ ★

How to Handle
A Psychic
Experience
page 35

Enquirer's New Santa Look-Alike Visits Children's Hospital

"Has Santa really come to see me?" wonders tiny Suzy Prieto as she stares up at Santa Look-Alike Charles Elledge. Suzy and dozens of other sick and lonely little children in a Miami hospital thrilled to the visit of The ENQUIRER's Santa, who come just to bring the youngsters a little Christmas cheer. (Story on page 29.)

"Enquirer's New Santa" National Enquirer™ December 23, 1975.

and the women who shopped at them. To enact his plan, standard journalist salaries were doubled to attract experienced writers and reporters. Two of his editors from the London Bureau, Iain Calder and William Dick, joined the New York editor Nat Chrzan and an editorial staff that was in constant flux as they developed a new style through trial and error. Sports were a turnoff to women shoppers, political issues created controversy, and explicit sex was considered pornographic. Each story, Pope said, had to appeal to more than 50 percent of its readers.

The *National Enquirer* Variety Package

The result of Pope's innovation was a diversified, relatively innocuous tabloid compared to its gore days, but one nonetheless designed to arouse an emotional response. As a tabloid, it retained the signature shock value, but even its tragic stories were given hopeful endings. The *National Enquirer* was not exactly the *Readers Digest*, but neither was it comprised of sex and violence.

The reader was regaled with rags-to-riches stories, hero awards, animal rescues, psychic predictions, medical breakthroughs, and gee-whiz anecdotes that would have made Joseph Pulitzer and William Randolph Hearst proud. Although less than half the content focused on celebrities, a celebrity romance earned first place on the front page. Eva Gabor revealed her secret fiancé, "I'm in Love, but Don't Tell Anyone Who He Is," and Jane Fonda showed a small military missile to Tom Hayden, "Henry Fonda: I Think Jane Will Be Happy with a Man like Him." To address the popularity of television, the *Enquirer* directed as much attention to television stars as to their counterparts in film. As the circulation sales increased, so did the consequent influence of the *Enquirer*, and celebrities' publicity agents frequently released selective and tantalizing information to a receptive audience.

NATIONAL
ENQUIRER
20¢
Vol. 46, No. 46, July 16, 1972

How 2 Minutes a Day Can Stop Backaches

Blaming Electric Utilities and Government, U.S. Senator Warns:

THE U.S. WILL ALMOST CERTAINLY HAVE A NUCLEAR DISASTER WITHIN 10 YEARS

...It Will Mean the Loss of Millions of American Lives

EXCLUSIVE!
1st Photos of
1973 Chevrolets
page 25

* * *

Why Does Robert
Vaughn Avoid
Seeing His Son?
page 14

* * *

Did These People
Glimpse Life
After Death?
page 19

* * *

Enquirer Story
Reunites 'Orphan'
With Mother
After 33 Years
page 2

* * *

An Intriguing
Look at Howard
Hughes' Dad
page 24

* * *

2 Days to Live —
Cancer Cured
By Faith Healer
back page

Jack Jones Sings 'I'm in Love Again'

For the fourth time in his 34 years, singer Jack Jones is crooning a new tune of love, this time with British actress Susan George, 21, shown here in happy harmony with Jack at a New York restaurant. Susan says "I don't want to see anyone else" and he admits "I love her so." (Interviews on page 3.)

"Jack Jones Sings 'I'm in Love Again'" *National Enquirer*™ July 16, 1972.

Lucky Dog

One of Generoso Pope Jr.'s favorite types of tale was the sentimental pet story. It seemed only natural, then, that the *National Enquirer* and its readers would have their very own pampered pet. The *Enquirer*'s psychic stars could not have predicted a more fortunate opportunity for an abandoned mutt than a life as Pope's Lucky Dog. Lucky, the winning name selected from a readers' contest, was a fuzzy black-and-white dog rescued from an animal shelter in Miami, Florida. He lived with former articles editor Joseph Cassidy, who considered Lucky his insurance against abrupt termination of employment in the *Enquirer*'s volatile job environment.

Lucky, the *Enquirer*'s lovable roving goodwill ambassador, was a frequent flyer. He traveled to Hollywood to play with Lassie and romped with President Nixon's dogs on the White House lawn. Never one to resist appealing to a soft spot in readers' emotions, Pope arranged a Christmas photo shoot for Lucky with actor Bob Hope in California. Hope dressed in a Santa Claus suit, and an amiable Lucky allowed himself to be placed into Santa's red felt bag. "Hope grunted slightly as he hoisted the 30-pound mutt in the sack over his shoulder," said Bob Temmey, the reporter assigned to the story. Temmey, hidden behind Hope so he would not be part of the photograph, positioned himself on his knees with his hands on the bottom of the sack supporting Lucky for the Christmas message, "Bob Hope and Lucky Team Up to Wish *Enquirer* Readers a Merry Christmas!"

A Public Relations Campaign

Prototypes followed by mass circulation issues demonstrated the new content and consequently reworked image of the *National Enquirer*. But promoting a tabloid in the supermarkets required more than a new image. Pope implemented an aggressive public relations campaign directed at supermarket executives by enlisting the aid of public relations expert Henry Dorman and former supermarket executive William Hall. Under their direction, the *Enquirer* lobbied supermarket associations, presented video programs, hosted celebrity-filled parties, and negotiated financial incentives. Pope proposed a sweet deal for the supermarkets: he guaranteed the sale of half the weekly issues he placed in the store. If fewer than half sold, Pope paid the store owner the difference between the anticipated and received income. He never had to pay.

Once the negotiations were successfully concluded, Pope allocated thousands of dollars for the construction of specially designed pedestal racks, all labeled *National Enquirer* and built to sit exactly at eye level on the checkout counter. By the latter part of the 1960s the *Enquirer* was in the supermarkets. Circulation grew from 75,000 in 1952 to 200,000 during the gore years to 700,000 in 1964. In 1970 the *Enquirer* sold close to two million copies a week.

Eventually, Pope joined the exodus to the suburbs. He relocated the editorial offices of the *Enquirer* to Englewood Cliffs, New Jersey, situating them across the Hudson River from Manhattan. The move to affluent Bergen County, known as the Gold Coast of New Jersey, was an indicator of Pope's success as well as a convenience. Here, a short drive from his residence, in a well-landscaped business park, the offices of the *Enquirer* faced the Prentice-Hall Publishing Company. The *Enquirer* continued to grow, but it was not until Pope moved the entire operation to Florida in 1971 that the *Enquirer* truly flourished.

Florida

Pope was not fond of traveling, but in 1969 he drove more than a thousand miles south on Interstate 95 to Pompano Beach, the site of the *Enquirer*'s printing plant, a low-cost, high-volume, non-union facility. Once a week semi-trailer trucks stopped in this small beach town, strategically located on the direct trucking route north from Miami, to load millions of copies of the *Enquirer* for distribution across the nation. Long-distance commercial carriers delivered their payload of manufactured goods from the industrial northeastern states to Florida, but as Florida was largely a tourist state and had little manufacturing, more goods flowed south than north. Usually the trucks returned north empty to pick up the next load, unless they could arrange a pick-up from Florida, called a back-haul. Any material picked up for a back-haul was trucked at a much reduced rate. Naturally, cost-saving measures interested Pope, and the *Enquirer* became part of a back-haul.

Inexpensive open land, low taxes, and a non-union work force were features of the past in Bergen County, New Jersey, but they were attractive incentives in South Florida at the time. Florida's business climate was as favorable as its subtropical weather and seductive life style.

Parallel to Interstate 95 in Pompano Beach is a slower highway, scenic route A1A, which follows the Atlantic Ocean along a coast of white sand beaches, blue sea, and palm trees. From Palm Beach south, A1A follows Florida's Gold Coast past modern resorts and Old Florida beach towns. Along this coastal road Pope discovered the fishing village of Lantana.

Lantana did not need wrap-around-glass condos, two-story yachts, or beachfront mansions to attract Pope. When Pope traveled to Lantana in 1969 it was home to working-class families and sun-seeking retirees. The pastel houses were mostly modest, one-story bungalows built out of Florida's favorite construction material, concrete block. Yellow and red hibiscus bushes the size of small trees lined the neat yards. The streets were quiet, the stores basic, and the people friendly. The Palm Beach Social Registry did not extend to Lantana and that suited Pope.

In Lantana Pope found what he was seeking, an unobtrusive place to work and live. East across the Intracoastal Waterway on the barrier island of Manalapan, Pope bought a house lot overlooking the ocean. In Lantana Pope negotiated his second real estate purchase, several acres of inexpensive commercial land bordering the railroad tracks. The stage was set for Lantana's most famous corporate resident. In New York City Pope's tabloid empire was born; in Lantana it thrived.

Chapter 3

Welcome to Florida, Welcome to the *National Enquirer*

ON A FRIDAY AFTERNOON in July 1971, the newsroom of the *National Enquirer* was quiet and empty; no phones ringing, no reporters cursing, no Page One conference. The *Enquirer* was en route from Englewood Cliffs, New Jersey, to Lantana, Florida. The following Monday morning the northern transplants walked into the custom-built *Enquirer* headquarters and blinked at the Florida sun streaming in through wide windows. Finding their desks, they returned to work.

The *Enquirer* editorial staff arrived in Florida with the completed page proofs of two advance issues, prepared in New Jersey and ready to go to press in Florida. The stories were selected for their timeless quality, but a few pages remained empty nonetheless for breaking celebrity news. The transition to the new work space went smoothly and the staff produced an entirely new weekly issue for Thursday distribution, eliminating the need for the preprepared copy. Eventually, one by one, the unused stories appeared in later issues.

Welcome to Florida

Welcome to Florida, the Sunshine State and land of healing sun, white sand beaches, blue waters, and temperatures that rarely drop below freezing. Florida is a paradise for tourists, winter escapees, beach bums, and homesteaders. But not everyone comes to Florida to lie on the beach or play golf; some seek a new beginning or a business opportunity.

Florida is kind to entrepreneurs. Its homestead exemption law protects a primary residence from bankruptcy while personal income is excluded from state taxes. Most significant to Generoso Pope Jr. was Florida's right-to-work law, which establishes that employment cannot be contingent on membership in a labor union or organization. Though he was not averse to paying decent wages and benefits, Pope vehemently opposed a unionized workforce, wanting total control of his enterprise.

In 1971, Walt Disney officially opened his innovative theme park on twenty-seven thousand acres of drained swampland in Orlando, a small agricultural community in central Florida. That same year, Generoso Pope Jr. relinquished the media center of New York City in favor of the fishing center of Lantana as the headquarters for his own innovation, the supermarket tabloid.

Geographically, Lantana is part of Florida's Gold Coast, a region which stretches along the Atlantic coast between Palm Beach and Miami and is known for its abundance of wealth and natural beauty. Yet economically and socially, Lantana was ignored in 1896 when Henry M. Flagler extended the Flagler Railroad south from St. Augustine to Palm Beach, the winter retreat for the wealthy and famous. Transported in luxurious railroad cars, prominent Northerners gathered for the winter at Flagler's Palm Beach Inn, the present-day Breakers. Twenty years later society architect Addison Mizner bypassed Lantana in favor of Boca Raton for the site of his extravagant resort that brought in Palm Beach's high society. The residents of Lantana shrugged and continued on their course as a quiet, little community that shunned industry, shopping malls, and pink condominiums.

Pope selected Lantana because it was exactly the place he had envisioned for the *Enquirer*, away from the distractions and pressures of

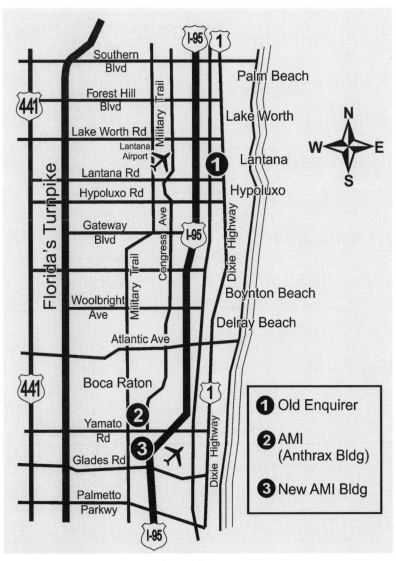

Palm Beach County Map. (Courtesy of Tom Wilbur.)

New York City. "We couldn't function properly at Englewood Cliffs. The moment you walked in the door, you were mad at the world, and everybody was mad at everybody. Down here they come in relaxed and happy," Pope said in an interview with journalist Malcolm Balfour.

In 1971 Lantana had one major industry, culvert manufacturing. The town offered one bowling alley, no movie theater; ample fishing supply shops, no trendy clothing boutiques. But it seduced visitors and residents with beautiful beaches, the warm ocean currents of the Atlantic Gulf Stream, and a subtropical climate only occasionally spoiled by the wandering hurricane. Generous paychecks safe from a state income tax enabled the *Enquirer* transplants to trade a two-room walk-up apartment in New York City for a house with a yard, palm trees, and a pool. When weary of sandals and shorts, the urbanites sought city lights a short road trip down Interstate 95 to Miami, or boarded a flight to London or New York City from the Palm Beach International Airport.

Once Pope moved to Lantana he rarely left Palm Beach County. He avoided air travel and devoted six days a week to the *Enquirer*. In five minutes, interrupted by one traffic light, he drove his late-model Chevrolet Impala from his ocean-front home on the barrier island of Manalapan to Lantana. He wore casual off-the-rack slacks, usually gray, and short-sleeved cotton shirts, except on Saturdays when he came to the office in black swimming shorts, a t-shirt, and flip-flops. A private person, Pope was left alone in Lantana to do his thing— mold and grow his company.

Pope took a gamble when he transformed the *National Enquirer* from a gory tabloid into one suitable for the supermarkets. His second gamble was moving to an out-of-the-way town in South Florida, miles and years away from the cosmopolitanism and synergy of New York City. Here in Lantana, Pope's phenomenal success with the *Enquirer* created a mecca for tabloid journalism. There would be no Tabloid Valley if Pope had not gambled and won.

Welcome to the *National Enquirer*

Surrounded by seven manicured acres of lawn, tall hedges, tropical trees, flowering shrubs, and garden beds, the *National Enquirer* faced Southeast Coast Avenue, a quiet side street in a working-class residential neighborhood. The back of the building bordered Federal Highway (U.S. Route 1) and a busy railroad track. Every Tuesday morning Pope stacked free copies of the weekly *Enquirer* in the alcove of the front entrance. Some residents were delighted. They were the first to know the latest gossip about Hollywood actors Liz and Richard—married, divorced, married again? Others, unimpressed by wealth or notoriety, ignored the presence of a famous tabloid. They would wait and see what the impact would be on their community. Of course, there were those, especially the New York snowbirds with long memories, who were aghast at the thought of a scandalous tabloid in town. But the sky did not fall and the sun continued to shine.

From the sidewalk, the *National Enquirer* looked like any nondescript red brick office building, identified by an illuminated commercial sign with the company's name and the outside temperature. Inside, the atmosphere was charged with the intensity of a true newsroom by a soft-spoken boss who instilled fear, power, and admiration, and by competitive editorial teams who were assessed through a demanding production rating system.

Generoso Pope Jr. managed every aspect of his publication, right down to the orders the gardener was given to trim the lawn to a height of exactly three inches. The *Enquirer* was built by Pope's vision, money, and energy. He was the ultimate entrepreneur, and jealously guarded his product by guaranteeing its quality. "Pope insisted on quality. He wanted it done right and wanted it done fast," said former production manager Barney Giambalvo.

Pope demanded competence, productivity, and allegiance as he aimed for his dream goal of making twenty million circulation sales in a week. As a reminder to his employees, both new and old, of the publication's success, Pope printed them T-shirts displaying its target circulation: "1971—1.5 Million." "1972—2 Million." "1973—3 Million." In 1976 the goal was a circulation of six million, so below these figures it read, "6 in '76." The average circulation that year came in at 5.9 million.

Pope dictated the hiring and firing, and his orders were then carried out by one of his editors. He fired the entire Public Relations Department when they wanted to unionize, and was rumored to have dismissed an assistant who poured him too much coffee, explaining, "Anybody who can't tell half a cup from a full cup is too stupid to work here." Reporters and editors who did not continually improve and increase their output of stories were either demoted or dismissed on the spot. In later years, Pope adopted the IBM Corporation's strategy and instead placed them on a 30-day probation. With the *Enquirer* making so much money, and a ready and willing supply of journalists waiting in the wings for the chance to earn unmatched paychecks and generous benefits, he could afford to be an exacting boss. Many dismissed reporters seized the opportunity to collect a sizable income as a freelancer for the *Enquirer* until Pope noticed their names once more on the payroll. He then instituted a "no Florida freelancers" rule that lasted one year.

The daily operations of finances, circulation, liability, advertising, and printing were delegated to experts, but Pope ran the editorial. He approved every story and photograph. From twenty or more story ideas submitted by each article editor every week, Pope selected which ones to pursue, choosing with an uncanny accuracy exactly what his readers wanted. On Saturday mornings Pope's barber acted as a sounding board for his ideas. If his barber wanted to know what happened off camera on the television series *All in the Family*, Pope figured the rest of the *Enquirer*'s readers would also. Once Pope or an editor dashed off a lead sentence, it was up to the reporters to produce a story that meshed with that lead. Usually the story idea was conceived before the result was obvious, unless the focus was a specific

The Old Royal Typewriter

"Pope didn't like computers," recalled assistant executive editor Larry Haley. "I was using an IBM PC during my tryout as an articles editor. Tryouts were tough. Most who tried out didn't make it." Articles editors had to produce their own story ideas, which then had to be approved by Generoso Pope Jr. Haley spent six weeks submitting hundreds of ideas, all of which were summarily ignored—not even given the recognition attendant to approval or rejection. He was failing miserably. "One day a security guard and I were in the Lantana office on Saturday," said Haley. "The security man noticed I was having trouble. He said, 'Why don't you get yourself an old typewriter and stop writing your story ideas on a computer?'" Haley borrowed a 1936 Royal typewriter from a junior photo editor who had inherited it from his grandfather. Early the next Saturday Haley was in his office typing on the old Royal machine. "After about an hour I looked up to see GP sitting at the desk next to me," said Haley. "He said, 'Tell me, why are you using that old typewriter?' I knew my cue and said, 'Mr. Pope, I know it sounds silly, but I get a clarity of thought by pounding these keys onto this paper that I can't get from that damned computer.'" By the next week, over 250 of Haley's leads were approved and he passed his tryout. "I didn't know then that GP hated computers and thought if I was smart enough to have figured that out without being told I was smart enough to be one of his editors." Haley bought the Royal from the photo editor for fifty dollars, "as a reminder of how strange my career has been."

target like the photograph of Elvis Presley laid out in his coffin, in which case the main story was approached from several angles.

For any given story, reporters submitted ten, twenty, and sometimes even thirty pages of detailed notes with quotes that researchers checked for accuracy. An evaluator looked for inconsistencies and then submitted a six-to-ten-line summary for Pope's approval. If approved, the story was condensed by the writers to conform to a page code assigned by Pope. A "vspp" rated a very short part page, while a "1T" earned the prime space at the top of the page. The rewrite was then returned to Pope for the final undisputed edict: "Kill" or "Passed, G.P.," penned in a red ink reserved exclusively for Pope's use.

Formula for Success

In January 1973, two years after the move to Lantana, the *National Enquirer* announced, "The *Enquirer* Tops 3,000,000. The *National Enquirer* Salutes Its Vast Family of Readers, the Men, Women and Children Who Are the Backbone of This Country." The company's formula for success was to pay close attention to its readers. "Constantly think of the readers. If you were reading the story, what would affect you?" said Pope. "Entertain, inform and touch people's hearts . . . this was the 'soul of the *Enquirer*,'" said former editor-in-chief Iain Calder.

Pope knew by instinct what a readers survey in 1980 confirmed: readers were drawn to the *Enquirer*'s stories because they triggered emotions. A cotton picker paid a scant 15-cents-a-day who went on to open a chain of discount stores and ultimately build a mansion with his huge profits inspired dreams—a miracle could befall anybody. A Hollywood star entering drug rehabilitation provoked contempt, but also elicited sympathy—after all, celebrities are as human as anyone else.

"The *National Enquirer* empowered its readers," said Calder. Every letter sent to the Reader's Service Department that requested information about "Breast Cancer Treatment—Biggest Breakthrough Ever," or expressed an opinion about stories like "Girls Who Dress like Boys Behave like Boys" was answered. The readers donated their time—"*Enquirer* Readers Help Knitters Provide Lap Robes for Disabled,"—and money—"Generosity of *Enquirer* Readers Opens Up a Whole New World for Little Donnie Mlynar." Overwhelmed by the volume of mail sent to the *Enquirer*'s specially created Reader's Service Department, the United States Postal Service assigned a designated zip code to the company's Lantana headquarters. "You have a good friend at the *Enquirer*," the publication told its readers.

"Why I Love America"

"Why do you love America?" the *National Enquirer* asked its youngest readers, the children of the supermarket shoppers. Malcolm Balfour, associate editor, wanted to elicit from the readers an idea that would rise to the top of Pope's feel-good story list. "Why I Love America" promised an upbeat ending, involved reader participation, and appealed to emotion. Children, the future of the nation, filled even the most cynical heart with at least the beginnings of patriotism, hope, and inspiration.

Balfour organized "Why I Love America" as a write-in contest. Over a period of several months the *Enquirer* published essays selected from the thousands of entries until two first-place winners, one boy and one girl, were selected. The grand prize was a trip first to the White House, where the winners met with President Ford, then to Disneyworld where they posed with Mickey Mouse. The response to the contest was so overwhelmingly enthusiastic that it was made an annual event, a "story with legs" that matured into a regular column, "What's Right with America," contributed by guest celebrities including actor Bob Hope and professional golfer Gary Player. Occasionally the *Enquirer* solicited more critical opinions that attempted to balance the glossy picture with a column titled "What's Wrong with America?" but the positive message was preferred.

Guiding Principles

Generoso Pope Jr.'s guiding principles combined sharp business sense and insight. Appeal to a broad range of readers with a variety of content. Pay the wages required to hire the best writers and reporters. Spend what was needed to get the story and get it first. Deliver with fierce workplace competition to keep employees at their best.

Superimposed from the top down was a team and rating system designed to stimulate competition and productivity. Typically, an editorial team consisted of a senior articles editor and an articles editor with one assistant, three to eight reporters, and a network of reliable freelancers and confidential sources. All teams reported to an executive editor who in turn reported to the editor-in-chief. Everyone, at all levels, was accountable to Pope.

The teams worked on dozens of stories at a time, influenced by a ten- to fourteen-day lead time. "Think of what people will be talking about two weeks from now," editor-in-chief Iain Calder told his editors. Articles editors, expected to generate at least thirty weekly story leads, gathered and evaluated ideas from newspapers and journals, international news services, reader's tip hotlines, stringers (freelancers), and inside sources. Their mission was to ensure their team met its quota of published stories. Editors vied for the most dependable and well-connected reporters, trying to secure those who could quickly produce a compelling story packed with interviews, emotional quotes, and colorful background details. As associate editor, Malcolm Balfour relied on two of his best senior reporters, Jim McCandlish and David Wright. "They ask every question imaginable to every person they can find. McCandlish charms with his Scottish brogue and exuberant personality; Wright, with his image of the perfect English gentleman, smartly dressed and polite."

Numbers were the goal. Colors were the code. A steady mix of tabloid stories was the result. On one wall was a scoreboard for reporters, while the opposite wall displayed a scoreboard for editors. Every week each group was rated according to its contribution. A full-page celebrity scandal scored a bright red or purple double-digit number, and the editor or reporter affiliated with it was catapulted to the lead and received a bonus. A brief advice column scored a mere one or two points displayed in a dull color like tan or grey. The contributor responsible for it slipped to last place. It was not quite the tabloid wars of London and Glasgow, but the pressure to perform was intense. "I got tired after seven years, wore out," Balfour said.

With such intense pressure to perform and a lack of job security, why did anyone work at the *Enquirer*? Excellent salaries and seem-

The Team Rating System

Until 1990, when the *National Enquirer's* corporate ownership instituted budget-cutting measures that eliminated editorial teams, the contributions of editors and reporters were monitored with a rating system devised by former editor-in-chief Iain Calder. "In many editorial offices politics and boozing companionship is the key to promotions. Bosses make assessments by watching and 'gut feel'—which is wrong," said Calder.

"The system was simple," he explained.

I had staff count every story and put clippings in folders. Editors would judge how much of a contribution a reporter had made to an individual story, e.g. 25 percent of the story. Each half year we would count out the numbers of each reporter and I would personally rate the quality and difficulty of the story going from "A" to "D." A major Page One might rate an "A" and a simple how-to could be a "D." One reporter might have 10 "D" stories and 2 "A" stories, etc. Another might have 6.25 "A" stories and 3.5 "D" stories. I would evaluate them on quality plus quantity.

A similar system applied to editors. "The system was responsible in part for the ability of our staff to get stories that others could not," said Calder.

ingly unlimited expense accounts played a large role in the decision, but equally enticing was the excitement of involvement in a successful new venture. Creativity and energy flowed through the newsroom, and news-gathering was an adventure, unrestrained by the limits often imposed in mainstream journalism, and certainly not boring.

Story Mix

Thirty-two pages filled with a variety of stories and presented in tabloid format in 1971 ballooned to more than sixty pages by 1980. The cover of a typical issue in 1973 highlighted for the readers what was inside. Center stage featured a large photograph of Hollywood actor Stella Stevens in the arms of her latest partner, above which was written, "Stella Stevens' Secret." A sensational headline spread across the top of the page, "Highly Respected British Interplanetary Society Reveals . . . Scientists Attempting Contact with an Alien Space Probe Believed to be Orbiting Earth." Alongside the celebrity photograph were "ears," narrow columns reserved for announcing the week's human interest stories, which offered a little bit for everyone—a ghost prevented actor Susannah York from purchasing her dream home, and it turned out astronaut Neil Armstrong was a recluse. Psychological advice made your life more interesting, while nutritional advice kept your family healthy, and a how-to article suggested ways to cut your food bill. A parental alert warned that television might retard the intellectual development of children, and yet celebrities revealed their favorite television shows in another story.

The variety of the content demonstrated that the success of the *Enquirer* stemmed from more than just celebrity gossip. The readers hoped for a celebrity exclusive but also expected their favorites: the rags-to-riches story, the hero award, "The *Enquirer* Doctor," a message from evangelist Billy Graham, and the weekly horoscope. The potential influence of a large, receptive audience did not escape the

Ari and Jackie

In the spring of 1973, Generoso Pope Jr. issued an edict to his editors and reporters: "Ari and Jackie are right here on our own doorstep. If we can't get an exclusive, then we're not worth a damn." Iain Calder, an articles editor at the time, said, "All the editors knew what he really meant was, 'If we can't get an exclusive, then all of you are not worth a damn.'"

Stories about former first lady Jacqueline Kennedy and her second husband Aristotle Onassis were one of the biggest sellers of the '70s, and this time the story was in the *Enquirer*'s backyard. While Jackie and Ari were visiting the Palm Beach social scene, they stayed on their yacht, anchored privately in the Intracoastal Waterway between West Palm Beach and Palm Beach. Fourteen reporters were assigned to stake out the yacht and canvass the local bars, restaurants, and hangouts to find an inside source. Jim McCandlish, a newly hired reporter, gained the confidence of a homesick Greek sailor. They met daily in out-of-the-way bars, McCandlish's apartment, and hotel rooms. At the conclusion of the interviews, the *Enquirer* ran double-page story spreads stretched out over three issues, unusual for the *Enquirer*, of life aboard the yacht. When the sailor decided to jump ship and return to Greece, the *Enquirer* funded his trip home.

notice of those who depended on public support or wanted to educate consumers. Congressional leaders submitted articles about whatever they wanted publicized—a proposed Senate bill or an example of government waste. The M.D. Anderson Cancer Center in Houston, Texas and the Arthritis Foundation reported their latest research to the *Enquirer* on the condition that they retain ultimate copy approval for the stories. This was the successful *Enquirer* of the 1970s, and this was what created a large family of loyal readers.

Roving Reporters

Pope did not hire foreign correspondents to collect stories; instead, he sent roving reporters to far-flung assignments, often for three or more months at a time, and usually in adventurous situations. It could be a wild idea or an international news event, but whether the effort produced a one-column story, a reject, or a major exclusive, Pope wanted quantity from which to select the best tabloid fare. Reporters traveled first class and were given tens of thousands of dollars in cash and a company credit card for the assignment. The funds available for confidential information and exclusive contracts were seemingly inexhaustible. "Money was regarded as something that just flowed in and was to be used to get the most interesting articles possible, regardless of the cost," said former reporter John Harris.

The Abominable Snowman

Always alert for stories about the abominable snowman—Bigfoot in North America, Yeren in China, Almasty in the Caucasus Mountains, Yowie in Australia, Yeti in Tibet and Nepal—the *Enquirer* learned from a news release by the Nepalese government of a Polish mountain-climbing team in the Himalayas who claimed they had taken photographs of Yeti tracks in the snow, and of a simultaneous claim that a

Yeti had attacked a Sherpa yak herder. Reporter Bob Temmey and a staff photographer were on assignment in India when they were immediately diverted to Kathmandu, Nepal to interview the mountain climbers, who had reportedly completed their expedition into the Himalayas and were off the mountain. As it turned out, they were ascending the mountain at the time.

"Don't expect to hear from me for 10 days," wired Temmey to the *Enquirer*, as he and his partner departed to try to overtake the mountain climbers. At 14,000 feet, altitude sickness forced the photographer to abandon the climb, but Temmey continued with just the Sherpa guides to the climbers' base camp at 17,500 feet. "Every muscle in my body ached, and my legs felt as if they had 50 pound weights tied to them," Temmey said. At night the temperature dropped to 30-below. Suffering from the effects of the high altitude, Temmey developed headaches and could not swallow solid food. His guide told him, "You have to go back, you're going to die." Temmey pressed on nonetheless and reached the 16-man climbing team at base camp, where he attained his hard-earned interview and photographs, "*Enquirer* Goes to Himalayas to Investigate New Evidence of . . . the Terror of the Abominable Snowman!"

Behind the Iron Curtain

Behind the Iron Curtain, Bill Dick and Henry Gris, two of the *Enquirer*'s intrepid editors, covered the Soviet Union's studies of paranormal phenomena. During the cold war, the Soviets calculated that the widely-read *Enquirer* was a perfect venue in which to advertise their studies, as its readership was intrigued by such experiments. For the *Enquirer*, the supervised visits and interviews were a golden opportunity to generate a steady flow of exclusive stories bound to sell papers. But stories about psychokinetic medium Ninel Kulagina, who claimed she could at will stop a frog's heartbeat, and Dr. Genaly

Sergeyev, who invented a time machine that could "recover the emotions and thoughts of people long since dead," were dropped in favor of a sex scandal traced from Moscow to Orlando, Florida.

In 1945, Zoya Fyodorova, a beautiful Russian movie star, had a love affair with Jackson R. Tate, a United States Navy admiral stationed in Moscow during World War II. Tate returned home to Florida and did not learn until 1963 that he had a daughter, Victoria, by Zoya. In 1975 Victoria contacted various members of the international press service in hopes that the publicity would pressure the Soviet Union into granting her a visa to visit her father. The *New York Times* wrote, "Soviet Child of War Wants to Visit U.S. Father," but it was the *Enquirer* that acted.

An American anthropologist who uncovered the story while living in Moscow spent almost fifteen years connecting Tate with his daughter—until the *Enquirer* appropriated the effort and secured the reunion in less than four months. After a series of negotiations in Florida and Moscow, the *Enquirer* obtained exclusive contracts with the admiral and his daughter and arranged a three-month visa for Victoria. The secret travel plans commenced.

Gris escorted Victoria, disguised in sunglasses, a wig, and a long baggy coat, onto a flight arranged a day earlier than scheduled from Moscow to Brussels, then to New York, and finally to Miami. In Miami two staff cars acted as decoys while an *Enquirer* reporter drove Victoria in a third car to a gated compound south of Palm Beach. There she was sequestered from an inquisitive media until the time of the reunion.

"It was like a fortress," said hair stylist Armando Giacosa, describing the high security at the secret hideaway. Summoned on a house call, Giacosa, fluent in several languages including French and Italian, packed his styling case and was chauffeured by an attractive woman in a black limousine to an undisclosed client at an undisclosed location. At no time were Victoria and Giacosa left unguarded. "A body-

"U.S. Admiral United With His Russian 'Love Child'" *National Enquirer*™ April 15, 1975.

guard even accompanied me to the store to buy extra hair products," he said.

Only after their own interview and photo shoot were complete did the staff at the *Enquirer* arrange a nationally televised press conference to introduce Victoria and Tate: "And the *Enquirer*—and only the *Enquirer*—was there to bring you these exclusive stories and photos." In an emotional reunion at the beach, "U.S. Admiral United with His Russian 'Love Child.' . .Tears streaming down her face, Victoria Fedorova cried, 'Papa!' and rushed into the arms of Admiral Jackson R. Tate, the father she had never seen."

The Search for Utopia

While roving editors Gris and Dick were immersed in intrigue behind the Iron Curtain, roving reporter John Harris lounged on a beach in Tahiti, embarked upon Pope's quest for utopia. His lead sheet read: "Is there really a Utopia left in this world? What's it really like to live in Tahiti and those other pipedream paradises? Let's send a reporter to write a series of articles."

For over four months, Harris island-hopped from the Scottish Isles to the South Pacific. Mingle with the natives, not the tourists, Pope said. Ask them, What is it like to live here? What do you worry about? What makes you happy? How do you earn a living? Harris hunted wild boar in Moorea. He escorted a date to a cremation party for a priest in Bali. On the way to a monastery in Hydra, he clung tightly to the neck of a mule as it zigzagged up a steep mountain trail, slipping occasionally on rocks, and even leaning over the side of a cliff to eat shoots of grass.

Once a week, Harris dispatched a new update regarding his search for utopia, describing in them secluded lagoons, spectacular waterfalls, white-sand beaches, and lush mountains on the one hand, but also traffic jams, beaches which were littered with beer cans, and areas choked with pollution and beset by poverty. With each account, Pope rejected yet another bid for utopia, his hopes for paradise shattered by the harsh realities of modern civilization.

Harris estimated the *Enquirer* spent one hundred thousand dollars on a trip that was calculated to produce months of entertainment for the readers and yield stories full of adventure and fantasies. Yet not one of Harris' stories was ever published. Pope did not deceive his readers; if the story did not live up to his expectations, he let it go.

The Brits

Harris, originally from a mainstream Ohio daily newspaper, said he was reluctant to take a job with the *National Enquirer* because he did not want the name of the "old guts and gore" or the "gossip rag" on his resume. But he could not resist the lure of travel, Florida sunshine, and a salary double the going rate for a mainstream newspaper journalist. Although the *Enquirer* recruited seasoned journalists from American newspapers, British journalists were Pope's favorites. They drew on the training they had received in the vibrant tabloid community of Great Britain to give the *Enquirer* a sharp competitive edge and to produce stories perfectly tailored to the supermarket tabloid. Pope said, "Bring 'em over, I want more of them."

Chapter 4

The Brits Are Coming

IN THE EARLY 1920s Finnish immigrants seeking sunshine and a piece of Florida real estate at a bargain land boom price settled in the Palm Beach County neighborhoods of Lake Worth and Lantana. Cuban exiles from Fidel Castro's revolution landed in Miami in 1959 and transported their culture to South Florida. In 1971 the initial contingent of British employees followed the *National Enquirer* from New Jersey to Florida. By the end of the decade, Tabloid Valley was home to a vibrant community of more than eighty tabloid journalists from England, Scotland, Ireland, Australia, and South Africa, known collectively as the Brits. They are ace reporters, sharp editors, and daring photographers, dedicated to practicing their craft in Tabloid Valley. They are the proud breed of Fleet Streeters.

Fleet Street

Fleet Street is a busy road in central London that connects the City of London to Westminster. Underneath the thoroughfare runs the subterranean Fleet River. In medieval times the river was wide, but with the demands of industrialization, the Fleet River dwindled to merely a narrow canal. Today the river runs beneath a covered drain that empties into the River Thames.

Historically, Fleet Street is a symbol of a dynamic tradition of news-gathering generated by the large, competitive publishing industry in Great Britain. In the early sixteenth century printing shops accumulated along Fleet Street because of the need for reproduction of legal documents for the nearby Inns of Court. Pubs congregated around the shops to accommodate the after-hours needs of the printers. It was not long before the concentration of printing presses in a central location attracted publishing businesses. From a second-floor office above the White Hart Pub, Edward Mallet published the first British daily newspaper, the *Daily Courant*, in 1702. By the beginning of the twentieth century Alfred Harmsworth, "the Napoleon of Fleet Street," established the picture tabloid as an important form of journalism in Great Britain.

Twentieth-century Fleet Street was headquarters for the most influential British newspapers. Yet in June 2005, the "last rites for Fleet Street" were held in St. Bride's Church, London. The street and its heritage survive, but the last remaining major news publisher, *Reuters*, joined its colleagues in the suburbs to take advantage of lower capital expenses and the additional space in which to expand their operations.

The Fleet Street tradition is rooted in a basic journalism tenet; get the news first and get it correctly. This sells newspapers. Tabloids are a vital part of the strong newspaper culture in Great Britain. It is not unusual for modern-day Londoners to buy two daily newspapers. For sober information about the state of the economy, they read the politically middle-of-the-road mainstream *Independent*. For sensationalist prose exposing a Royal Family scandal, they read the "biggest and brightest" *News of the World* tabloid.

Motivated by competition from a half dozen British tabloids, Fleet Streeters track down a hard news story as ferociously as a celebrity rumor. "Kill or be killed," said Scottish reporter Jim McCandlish. They always return to the newsroom with a story, even if it is not the one they set out to find. There are no excuses; complete the job or go work for a backwater newspaper. If the lead they intend to follow does not materialize, reporters develop another angle or an entirely different story. They then head for their favorite pub to socialize with their comrades from competing papers.

Traditionally, Fleet Streeters serve a tough apprenticeship which can last as long as seven years. Former *National Enquirer* editor-in-chief Iain Calder is a graduate of the "Heavy Mob," a team of formidable investigative reporters at one of the oldest and most widely read Scottish tabloids, the Glasgow *Daily Record*. "That anything-goes climate was the best preparation possible for a career with Gene Pope and the *National Enquirer*," said Calder.

"Anything Goes"

In 1960, the city of Glasgow, Scotland, was the scene of "anything-goes" newspaper circulation wars that produced reporters who "performed the impossible or played the most ingenious dirty tricks on the opposition," said former *National Enquirer* editor-in-chief Iain Calder. Calder was responsible for at least one devious diversion himself. On assignment to interview a family, he was the first reporter to arrive at their home, but not far behind him came rival reporters. Needing time and privacy, Calder described the metaphorical media wolves (himself excluded) at the family's door and persuaded them to allow him to drive them to a relative's house. He placed a note on the door, "Gone to 2004 North Street, Paisley," which was a fake address thirty minutes in the opposite direction.

Pope and the Fleet Streeters

The British invasion of the *National Enquirer* began when Generoso Pope Jr. brought the London Bureau editors Iain Calder and Bill Dick to New York City; the same period during which the *Enquirer* was transitioning from covering gore to a more acceptable variety of stories. Soon after, Calder and Dick recruited some of their colleagues from back home, but the largest migration occurred after the *Enquirer* evolved into a supermarket tabloid and moved to Lantana. Word traveled quickly among friends about a tabloid in sunny Florida whose pay was far above industry standards and that was interested in hiring British staff. Pope understood distribution and readership; the Fleet Streeters understood news-gathering. Admittedly, the *Enquirer* staff rewriters in New York needed to be on the alert for a British colloquialism: "I was so surprised, I fell across the bonnet of my car, said an Alabama sheriff when he spied a UFO." A small price to pay, Pope thought, for a complete tabloid package delivered by the Brits, a package boasting tight and crisp sentences, colorful background details, supporting quotes, and photographs, all working together to create a gripping story.

Job Tryouts

A typical job tryout for the *National Enquirer* was presented as a working vacation, all expenses paid, at the beach. The interview process was loosely structured and the rules were vague and capricious, but the tryout always involved sharing the newsroom workload. A prospective articles editor sorted through hundreds of archived news clips for story ideas that hopefully would catch Pope's fancy. A one-sentence story lead tested a reporter's ingenuity and perseverance. The tryout period might last a morning, a week, or a month, at the end of which the British recruits either returned with a suntan to the cold drizzle of London or bought an American-sized convertible with a Florida license plate.

Joe West arrived from the training fields of the Glasgow *Daily Record* and the London *Daily Mirror* for a tryout in Lantana. Before he had time to unpack and savor the sunshine, an articles editor handed him thousands of dollars in cash and a plane ticket to Fort Dodge, Iowa.

The lead sentence focused on a farmer who claimed a UFO had landed in his soybean field, leaving behind a charred triangle coated in a tar-like substance. Scientists presented logical theories for the phenomenon, but the farmer and a self-proclaimed UFO proponent from the pop culture capital of UFO's, Roswell, New Mexico, held to their belief that an alien aircraft had landed there. West wrote the story according to what the *Enquirer* readers wanted to believe—that is, that an alien invasion was possible—and dispatched it to the home office in Lantana. For two weeks West, with plenty of money and not too many places to spend it, waited in Fort Dodge for a response from Lantana.

After the two weeks were up, West called Lantana only to have an editorial assistant there tell him to "hang loose," which he did for one more week. His next phone call to the *Enquirer* revealed that his articles editor had been promoted, and West, lost in the shuffle, was left with no editor. Again, he was told to "hang loose." Another week later and thirty days from the start of his assignment, he once again called the home office. Reassigned to a different articles editor, the UFO story abandoned, West was ordered back to Florida. He was hired.

Tabloid Ploys

The Fleet Streeters imported by the *National Enquirer* group and later by *Star* and Globe Communications had few reservations about writing for a tabloid, especially ones that paid so well and offered an opportunity to live at the beach. News-gathering methods that journal-

"Dummies"

Even the most experienced journalist had to prove his or her worth to Generoso Pope Jr. Before the *Weekly World News* became affectionately known as the "Wacky World News" for its fabricated stories, Pope intended his newly created tabloid to be informative, featuring offbeat but true news stories. In 1979 Phil Bunton, a Fleet Streeter previously with the *Star* and the *New York Post*, was recruited by Pope for the position of editor. But he had to pass the test: create a fake magazine, a dummy, complete with short entertaining stories as well as corresponding potential headlines and photographs that would demonstrate his aptitude for tabloid-style journalism. Although the stories Bunton researched and wrote were never used, Pope picked him as the inaugural editor of the *Weekly World News*.

ists elsewhere might consider unethical were an essential part of the game to those working in Tabloid Valley. They added a thrill to the chase and allowed a maneuvering for advantage over rivals. When there was a problem to be solved—how to stymie and thereby beat the opposition—it was attacked with tabloid ploys.

"When I was editor," said Mike Foley, University of Florida journalism professor and previously executive editor of the *St. Petersburg Times*, "we did not pose to get a story. It was former editor Gene Patterson's belief—and I came to agree—that you couldn't lie to get a story and expect readers to believe you started telling the truth when you sat down to write the story." But undercover reporting is considered a legitimate tactic by the tabloids to access a story, particularly if a celebrity is involved. How else could the *Enquirer* attend actor Bing Crosby's funeral? Certainly not by invitation. An oft-told reporter's story—with as many embellishments as variations—tells of a bogus

"Father Francis" who passed through the receiving line with a tape recorder in the pocket of his clerical robe. Father Francis played his role so well that he was invited to be interviewed by a local television station, a public appearance he judiciously declined. Encouraged by his successful impersonation, he circulated among the guests. "Father Francis," he introduced himself to another priest. "Damn it, what's wrong with you, it's me, Vin," answered an *Enquirer* photographer, there to snap a picture of the coffin lowered into the ground.

Checkbook journalism, considered unethical by most mainstream journalists, ties up an exclusive interview and builds the critical list of confidential contacts that is hoarded by each reporter and editor. Once an actor, politician, or billionaire achieves fame, the payroll of the supermarket tabloids expands to include certain well-placed sources: the celebrity's chauffeur, housecleaner, hair stylist, a bartender at a favorite restaurant, or courthouse clerks.

But competitiveness and ingenuity, at least as much as cash in their pockets, give the Fleet Streeters the edge. "You are only as good as your next story," said reporter Jim McCandlish. Fleet Streeters compete as if their job depends on it. And so it did, in the Fleet Street tabloid wars and in Pope's domain.

Fleet Streeters in Florida

Malcolm Balfour, a British South African respected for his integrity and professionalism as an international journalist, caught Pope's attention when Balfour interviewed him for a news article. In 1972 Balfour was in Miami on assignment as a freelance journalist when he learned about a New Yorker who had moved to the little-known town of Lantana and was making millions of dollars selling a tabloid in supermarkets. Who was the man behind the *National Enquirer*, a tabloid that did not require an attraction like the London *Sun*'s topless "Page 3 Girl" to sell papers?

Balfour's interview was ignored by the local press. Not surprisingly, in spite of record-breaking sales as a supermarket tabloid, the new *Enquirer* had trouble living down its past notoriety in the eyes of the mainstream Florida press. Local newspapers did not want to advertise the presence of a sensational tabloid in Florida by publishing Balfour's article. The rest of the nation, though, was watching Pope redefine the tabloid industry, and *Reuters* international wire service bought the story. Consequently, readers all the way from Washington, D.C., to Balfour's home city, Johannesburg, South Africa, read "*Enquirer*: Violence Gets the Ax." The world took note of Pope, and Pope of Balfour.

Two months later Balfour became an associate editor for the *National Enquirer*, bought a home in Lantana, and hosted a séance in his dining room. Seated around the table were psychic Jeane Dixon, Balfour and his wife, and three Fleet Street colleagues. While Dixon communicated with spirits, the Brits took notes by candlelight to enlighten the *Enquirer*'s readers.

Psychic phenomena were popular in the 1970s and guaranteed readers' interest in the *Enquirer*. Among the charismatic psychics who gained celebrity status as television personalities was Uri Geller, who claimed he could bend metal spoons, stop or start clocks, and duplicate drawings and images through extra sensory perception. Prove it to the *Enquirer* readers, Balfour challenged Geller.

Uri Geller Goes Airborne

"Does Uri Geller Have Psychic Powers? You Can Find out by Taking Part in the Biggest Test Ever." A mail-in coupon for the *Enquirer*'s readers included space to record their experience with Geller's professed powers as he soared airborne in a hot air balloon to conduct psychic experiments. The hot air balloon was Balfour's personal touch, thrown in for dramatic effect.

On August 30, 1975, Geller's balloon lifted off from a field in southern New Jersey near Princeton. He was accompanied by an *Enquirer* reporter unhappy at the prospect of "going up in a balloon full of holes." Fifteen hundred feet above earth at exactly 5 p.m. eastern standard time, Geller concentrated for ten minutes on repairing a broken watch or electrical appliance. At 5:15 p.m. he concentrated on creating two simple drawings. Ten minutes later, he focused his thoughts on a two-digit number. While Geller floated in the balloon interpreting energy waves, the *Enquirer* instructed readers at the appointed times to concentrate on a watch or toaster they wanted repaired, sketch a simple line drawing, preferably one that evoked pleasant thoughts, and select a number.

The balloon landed, a euphoric Geller jumped out to be photographed, and a relieved reporter crossed the field clutching a facsimile of an Egyptian jar that contained Geller's secret predictions. The jar was placed in a lockbox for the return trip to Lantana.

An inundated Reader's Service Department in Lantana and a cooperating newspaper in Great Britain received thousands of readers' responses sent from the United States and Europe. Pope, to confer credibility, formed a committee that included a Catholic priest and a sheriff's officer to oversee the processing of the responses.

As it turned out, there was no need for worried reporters to stuff the ballot box to ensure a favorable outcome and earn themselves bonus points. "Uri Geller Beats Incredible Odds in Spectacular ESP Experiment." A surprisingly large percentage of the readers' answers corresponded to the correct number, fifty-seven, and a drawing of a tree. Almost half the people reported that a broken watch or appliance now worked. "I felt incredible psychic vibrations up there," Geller told the *Enquirer* readers, "It was the most exciting thing I ever took part in."

Uri Geller Beats Incredible Odds In Spectacular ESP Experiment

By DICK SAXTY

In the most spectacular ESP experiment ever, famed psychic Uri Geller achieved an incredible success that defied odds of "more than 10 billion to one," say astonished experts.

As Geller soared in a balloon high over Princeton, N.J., people all over America and across the Atlantic received telepathic messages he transmitted in a dramatic test sponsored by The ENQUIRER.

PSYCHIC Uri Geller — his success amazed mathematicians and researchers.

"The only conclusion I can come to is that Uri Geller has extraordinary psychic powers. The results are simply incredible," declared an amazed Dr. James Boyette, distinguished mathematician at the University of Florida.

Readers had been asked to take part in a three-part experiment by an article in The ENQUIRER's August 26 issue and also in a cooperating British newspaper.

They were advised that Geller would begin the first experiment at 5 p.m. Eastern Daylight Time on August 30 by concentrating for precisely 10 minutes on repairing broken watches and appliances. Readers were asked to concentrate along with him.

At 5:15 p.m., readers were told, Geller would concentrate for 5 minutes on two simple drawings, and readers were asked to try to pick up his thought waves.

Finally at 5:35 p.m., Geller would focus on a two-digit number, and readers were asked to tune in on his telepathic transmission.

Readers were requested to use a coupon that accompanied the article to record their results — and send them to The ENQUIRER or to the British newspaper.

The coupon had spaces to reproduce the two-digit number and the pictures Geller transmitted.

There was also a space to jot down whether there was any success in repairing broken items.

A total of 4,041 readers responded.

Astonishingly, 308 people came up with the correct two-digit number — which was 57. At the same time, 798 people got one of the drawings — a tree.

And 448 got the other one — a car.

Additionally, 28 people correctly picked up two of the psychic messages.

Twenty one had a combination of a tree and the number 57, while six had the car and 57, and one had the car and tree.

And 1,851 people — almost half the total who responded — reported that Geller helped them repair broken watches and appliances.

The odds are astronomical that 308 people of the 4,041 entries would get the two-digit number.

The odds are actually "more than 10 billion to one," revealed Dr. Boyette, who used a computer to analyze the results.

"Geller must have incredible

just incalculable. Simply fantastic.

"Geller appears to have performed the impossible as far as science and mathematics are concerned."

Leo Katz, executive director of the Institute of Mathematical Statistics — a professional society of mathematicians and statisticians associated with Michigan State University — told The ENQUIRER:

"I'm completely astonished by these results. The odds against so many people getting the drawings correct are astronomical. It is truly astounding."

Dr. Harry K. Panjwani, researcher in medicine and psychiatry at Rockefeller University in New York, told The ENQUIRER:

"Pure chance could not explain the tremendous numbers of people who were somehow psychically plugged in to Geller while he floated in the balloon."

In Britain — thousands of miles away from the site of the experiment — 1,123 people sent in responses to the weekly newspaper Réveille, which had agreed to participate in The

ica. I think you have proven that Mr. Geller really does have some strange power we can't explain.

"It's particularly staggering that people in Britain, so many miles away from Geller, could have picked up his messages.

"I would agree that the odds are more than 10 billion to one that so many people would come up with the two-digit number."

Enthusiastic readers also wrote in from Canada, Mexico, Bermuda and every state in the nation.

Overjoyed by the spectacular success of the balloon experiment, Geller told The ENQUIRER:

"I knew the experiment would work.

"I felt incredible psychic vibrations up there. It was the most exciting thing I ever took part in.

"I'm naturally thrilled at the fantastic results. I have always wanted to test my powers in a transatlantic experiment, and I know that this was the biggest ESP experiment ever held anywhere."

HIGH IN BALLOON, Geller stands in center of gondola with the pilot and an Enquirer reporter.

ENQUIRER's experiment.

Of these people, 53 correctly picked the two-digit number, 119 drew the tree, and eight the car.

Watches and appliances were reported fixed by 280.

Prof. John Taylor, head of the mathematics department at King's College in London, England, told The ENQUIRER:

"I am amazed by the results both here and in Amer-

"And although there is no possible way in which a computer could calculate the odds against people getting his drawings correct, the results of that experiment are also fantastic.

"When you think of the astronomical number of different shapes in the world that could have been drawn, the odds are

THESE SKETCHES, penned by Geller in the balloon, were copied by hundreds of readers, who apparently picked up the psychic's thought waves.

Waking Up Suddenly From Deep Sleep Can Turn Normal People Into Killers, Warns Psychiatrist

A little-known phenomenon called "sleep drunkenness" can push normal people into irrational acts of violence — including murder, warns a top psychiatrist.

"I have documented 20 cases of murder and 30 cases of other crimes that can be attributed to sleep drunkenness — the confused state which follows sudden awakening from a deep sleep," said Dr. Alexander Bonkalo, professor of psychiatry at the University of Toronto.

"Not enough attention has been paid to this phenomenon, especially in recent times when many ordinary citizens are going to sleep with loaded guns handy.

"What they fail to realize is that if they fall asleep fear-

ful that they may be the victims of an intruder, they can be a real danger if they are suddenly aroused.

"There is a good possibility they'll use the weapon on whoever is closest — even a beloved spouse or child."

Said Dr. Regis Riesenman, a psychiatrist at Arlington, Va.:

"Up to 10 years ago we didn't have to worry about sleep drunkenness. But these days people are going to sleep with all kinds of fears on their minds.

"When such people buy a gun and keep it handy for their protection and are then awakened abruptly, there is a great likelihood that they'll grab that gun and shoot it be-

fore they're fully conscious.

"Even if the sleeper doesn't have a gun handy he could be extremely violent and dangerous if he is a fearful person and wakens suddenly. He could take a swing at you."

Added Dr. William Chapman, professor of psychiatry

at the University of Virginia in Charlottesville: "These are violent times and people who seek to protect themselves from intruders in their homes by keeping weapons close at hand should be alerted to the fact that they are placing their families in more danger than they face from potential intruders."

— DENNIS D'ANTONIO

People Supported by Tax $$ Outnumber Workers In Private Enterprise

More people are being supported by tax dollars in the U.S. than there are workers in private enterprise to support them, according to Ford Motor Co. economists.

In 1974, the economists said, 80.6 million Americans were dependent on tax dollars for their income. These included

the unemployed, people on welfare, retirees and the disabled, military personnel and government workers.

But at the same time, there were only 71.6 million persons employed by the private sector of business.

Sheik Brian Hogan

In every Fleet Streeter there is a bit of audacity. Brian "Hogie" Hogan, an Australian, was "a hell of a character" and a master at disguises. No matter how trivial the caper, he provided the *National Enquirer* readers with entertainment. Somehow, Hogan persuaded the authorities at the Baltimore Zoo to permit him to don a gorilla suit, occupy an empty cage, and cavort for the visitors. He was the gorilla extraordinaire until a child shouted, "A blue-eyed gorilla!"

Hogan's opportunity to please Pope presented itself when Pope issued the broad directive that he wanted a government exposé. Hogan traded a gorilla costume for an Arab robe and head cloth. He intended to test the security in the United States Senate office building in Washington, D.C., and craft a hard news story, gathered tabloid style. Since the government courted the Arab countries for oil resources, Hogan concluded an Arab sheik would be welcomed by the senators.

After a few select purchases at a Georgetown costume store, Hogan metamorphosed into the Sheik Ongha Biran—an anagram of Brian Hogan—a citizen of Hilat Al-Bhundi, a fictitious country. Backed by the *Enquirer's* expense account, he rented a black limousine, driven by a colleague posing as chauffeur and interpreter.

At the first checkpoint, the private parking lot, the guard nodded and waved him through to a visitor parking space. At the second checkpoint, the front entrance, the guard only glanced peremptorily at his identification. Hogan was inside the building. As he roamed from office to office, he smiled, chatted in a language of strung-together gibberish, and posed for photographs with senators and their secretaries. No one asked for credentials until an Arab-American senator recognized the bogus dialect. Caught, Hogan was evicted, but with a story. A year later, Hogan returned to the Senate office building, but this time, he did not get past the parking lot. Senate security was addressed.

The Valley of Longevity

The Fleet Street tabloid journalists thrive on diversity and adventure. "Don't know when (as always) I'll be back but that's the way this life goes (and who could complain?)," said reporter Jim McCandlish. In 1973, McCandlish, who reported from sea Greenpeace's first nuclear protest expedition to Amchikta Island in Alaska, was in Rio de Janeiro, Brazil, recovering financially and physically from a six-month backpacking trip through South America and down the Amazon River. When the *Enquirer* offered an all-expenses-paid trip to Ecuador, fifteen thousand dollars for walk-about money, and a story lead fit for an adventurer, he accepted.

Five thousand feet above sea level in a remote area of southern Ecuador is a valley called Vilcabamba, the Valley of Longevity, where a preponderance of indigenous people live to be well over a hundred years old. Find them, said Pope, learn their secret. They looked old, he said, but why did they not act old? International geneticists, gerontologists, anthropologists, and now one reporter from the *Enquirer* undertook the arduous journey to reach Vilcabamba.

From the coast of Rio de Janeiro McCandlish traveled by first-class jet to Lima, Peru, where he transferred to a single-engine plane which took him into the interior of Ecuador. There he rented an open-air jeep to continue his journey deep into the remote regions of the lower Andes Mountains. Before going far, the primitive track gave way to a narrow, ancient Inca trail, at which point he traded the jeep for a burro to carry him through thick cloud forests, up mountain paths, and across pedestrian rope bridges that spanned deep river ravines. For the last part of the trip he walked to meet the old people.

The centenarians had wrinkled faces, missing teeth, and diminished hearing, but they climbed mountains, plowed fields, smoked cigars, drank rum, and danced and flirted at festivals. It is the water, they claimed; the mineral water was healthy. Additionally, the climate was mild and they ate healthy, organic foods from their orchards, vegetable gardens, and pasture-fed animals. They were a happy people surrounded by friends and family. Here was Pope's simplistic, singular approach—how to live longer, reduced to a few easy steps.

Pope demanded proof of age and happiness: photographs, interviews with quotes, and all this backed up by expert opinions, condensed for the *Enquirer* readers to one- or two-sentence references from scientific studies. McCandlish climbed a mountain to an isolated monastery perched on a cliff where a parish priest produced faded baptism certificates. Through an interpreter, he collected testimonies that told of, among other wonders, a recent father who claimed to be 127 years old and a 110-year-old woman who threaded a needle without eyeglasses. He hired a local photographer who produced rolls of film that, when developed, inexplicably showed a black line through the middle of every photo. "The Oldest People in the World!" was a terrific read for the *Enquirer*'s fans.

Gig Young Dies and Peter Falk Shines

One Fleet Streeter is a challenge; a team of Fleet Streeters comprises a daunting force. In October 1977, editor-in-chief Iain Calder borrowed a tactic from the Glasgow *Daily Record*. He organized a contest between two editorial teams dispatched to New York City to compete for stories. The rules were, first, that the stories had to originate from the New York City news scene, and second, that they be fact-based, verified by the research department. Winner takes the glory, a cash bonus, and job security for at least one more month.

The lead editors contrasted in style and approach. Malcolm Balfour, a Brit from the male-dominated Fleet Streeters, was pitted against an American woman journalist, Shelley Ross. Each editor selected their best staff reporters and freelancers for the assignment. Although Balfour's team consisted of a preponderance of Fleet Streeters, a couple of Brits joined Ross's team to balance out the competition.

First on the scene were Ross and her team, who arrived early in the week to get a jump start on the Brits. Balfour and his team arrived the following weekend to explore the sights and pubs of New York City. On Monday morning the American team submitted a week's worth of ideas. The Brits had none; it was time for them to get to work. By the middle of the week, both teams were locked in fierce competition for New York stories.

A psychic client list, inventions inspired from dreams during sleep, and pampered Manhattan pets pacified the home office for a short time, but soon they wondered: where was the sensational celebrity story? Ordinarily, an aging, bypassed actor like Gig Young would not be considered Page One material. But after three weeks of marriage, Young, 64 years old, allegedly shot his fifth wife, who was 31 years old, and then committed suicide in their Manhattan apartment. Rumors circulated about sexual incompatibility, alcoholism, depression, and even a murder/suicide pact. The *Enquirer* readers wanted to know: what was going on between Gig and his wife that led to their violent deaths? Why did Gig do it?

After efficiently dispatching the question of what happened, the two separate teams fixed their sights on unearthing the private lives of Young and his wife. Ross's team produced exclusive wedding photos. Luckily, Balfour's team resurrected an interview with Young taken by a team member a few weeks before the murder. It was not a Page One story, but it earned the Brits ample points in the New York competition. They headed for the racetrack to celebrate. Cell phones were not prevalent in 1977, and racetracks restricted phone use to control betting, so Balfour was unavailable when Calder called from Lantana with a different angle on the Gig Young story. David Wright, the only reporter on the team still at the hotel, paged Balfour at the racetrack, "Call Iain Calder NOW." Balfour was resigned yet pragmatic, "Oh, that's it, I'm going to get fired—we'll just see this race."

Putting any story on the back burner, even just for a bit of fun, was not acceptable at the *Enquirer*. But the damage was done, the night young, and the expense account intact. The Brits began their evening and good fortune befell them at the Carlyle Hotel piano bar. At the bar a well-known television newscaster embraced a beautiful blonde who was not his wife. Jay Gourley, an American reporter on the team, snapped two "gotcha" photographs and the Brits ran out the door. They were partially redeemed in Lantana.

Their next strategic move was dinner at a five-star Italian restaurant frequented by celebrities and bound to provide an opportunity for an impromptu interview. Fleet Street camaraderie is infectious. Seated at the table next to the reporters was Peter Falk, star of the television series *Columbo*, who was attracted by the good cheer of the Brits and took the opportunity to share his thoughts about astrology, marriage, and food—all the personal gossip that the *Enquirer*'s readers eagerly read in "Peter Falk's Five Rules for a Happy Marriage." The Brits did it again, surviving with fly-by-the-seat-of-your-pants, quick-thinking Fleet Street journalism.

Pope relied on the Brits to help propel his tabloid to its prime position in the marketplace, but he built the *Enquirer*'s model and made it into a reality. Mike Nevard, a Brit who served in various editorial capacities at the *Star*, the *Enquirer*, and the *Globe*, said,

> From early beginnings in New York, Pope created a weekly black-and-white newspaper that combined elements of U.S. scandal magazines like *Whisper, Hush-Hush* and *Confidential*, with the brash format of British daily tabloids, like the *Daily Mirror* and later the *Sun*, with more than a little help from British newspapermen he imported to make it all work. The original blood-and-guts approach was dropped in favor of front page headlines like "Adam and Eve Were Astronauts" when the *Enquirer* broke new ground by going into supermarkets—a brilliant move that pushed circulation to around 5 million.

From his London vantage point, media mogul Rupert Murdoch observed Pope's success. Both men sold papers. Both men wanted to

The Blue Anchor Pub

Lee Harrison, a former *National Enquirer* reporter and *National Examiner* editor from Liverpool, England, said, "My tabloid years were the best days of my life. I'm glad I lived through it." What does a Fleet Streeter do for an encore after undertaking "swashbuckling" news-gathering for the supermarket tabloids? He buys a pub.

In 1995 Harrison and tabloid colleague Roy Foster opened the Blue Anchor Pub on East Atlantic Avenue in Delray Beach. The exterior is made up of the orig-

inal façade from a historical pub in London's Chancery Lane; complete with English oak and stained glass windows. "The very same doors you entered today were well known to Winston Churchill. As a young Fleet Street journalist and Member of Parliament in the early 1900s, he often dropped by the old Blue Anchor for a pint!"

To Fleet Streeters, a pub is as essential as the newsroom. Generoso Pope Jr., understanding the value of brainstorming sessions, sponsored martini lunches for his editors, and at five o'clock he sent the reporters to The New England Oyster House or the Hawaiian Ocean Inn for free drinks so they could continue their workday in compatible surroundings.

When the supermarket tabloids became one corporate entity, Tabloid Valley attracted a different breed of reporters and editors who spent less time on the road and more time in the office chasing stories by phone or the Internet. Little League games replaced after-hours pub meets.

But in 2001, after an anthrax-dusted letter contaminated the AMI building in Boca Raton, tabloid journalists gathered at the Blue Anchor Pub to regroup and fill in the information gap left by the FBI's investigation. Once again, the Blue Anchor Pub became a center of Tabloid Valley camaraderie.

Blue Anchor Pub, Delray Beach, Florida. (Courtesy of Lee Harrison.)

win. In the 1960s Murdoch, who began his publishing career in his native Australia, was the rising star of the British media world. By the 1970s his acquisitions included two popular British tabloid newspapers, the *News of the World* and the *Sun*. After a brief news publishing experiment in 1974 in San Antonio, Texas, Murdoch relocated his North American base of operations to New York City and announced, "A Great New Star Is Rising!" Murdoch launched the *National Star* weekly tabloid with a flashy television promotional campaign, "$5M. Boost on TV." He intended to compete with the *National Enquirer*. Tabloid Valley was beginning to impact more than just a small stretch of beach in Palm Beach County, Florida.

Chapter 5

The Rise of Tabloid Valley

THE *National Enquirer* was making a splash in the tabloid industry; it could no longer hide uncontested in Lantana. Australian-born British media mogul Rupert Murdoch recognized the *Enquirer* as a shrewd business investment and a quick way to break into the American tabloid market. He reportedly offered to buy the *Enquirer*, but Pope declined to meet, harboring no intention of selling the company he had built. Murdoch did not go away, however. In 1974 he challenged Pope by introducing the weekly *National Star*, "the world's most sparkling newspaper," founded in the *Enquirer*'s birthplace, New York City. Multi-million dollar television commercials announcing the advent of a new supermarket tabloid specifically targeted the *Enquirer*'s readers.

The first issue of the *National Star*, later shortened to the *Star*, was loosely modeled after Murdoch's British tabloids, intended to attract men with "*Star* packed sports action," women with "*Star* packed picture power," and teenagers with "the *Star*'s pop music and entertainment pages." The approach failed miserably with the American supermarket crowd. Within two weeks, the *Star* changed its editorial content and style to focus on women. It eliminated its coverage of sports and politics and concentrated its energies and resources on celebrity news.

"Ex-Miss World Says Tom Jones Was 'Just a Good Friend'" *National Star*™ March 16, 1974.

The *Star*, selling predominantly celebrity gossip, shared rack space at the supermarket with the *National Enquirer*, selling Pope's unique mix of stories. While the *Enquirer* was proud to be a tabloid in newsprint black and white, the *Star* strove to look more like a magazine, covering itself with colored newsprint and white or yellow headlines displayed against a bright blue background. Stylistic choices aside, both tabloids were after the same goal: exclusives.

The *Enquirer* continued to dominate the breaking-news scene by having an excess of editors, reporters, and photographers equipped with a ready stash of cash and established contacts, but two or three *Star* reporters worked efficiently and aggressively to remind the *Enquirer* that the *Star* was a real contender for national supermarket sales. In 1977, the *Star* produced its first all-time bestseller, "Exclusive: Read the Book the World Is Talking About," which sold over 3 million copies.

The successful, exclusive story that sold out the *Star* was a serialized version of *ELVIS: WHAT HAPPENED?*, a book authored by Steve Dunleavy and based on the stories of three of Presley's bodyguards. The *Star* expected a piece about Elvis to be popular, but it could not foresee the circumstances that ultimately created such phenomenal sales. The month the book was published, halfway through the *Star* series, Elvis died. An entertaining story suddenly became important as well.

In August of 1977 Elvis Presley collapsed on the bathroom floor of his Graceland mansion in Memphis, Tennessee. Was the cause of death an overdose of prescription drugs? Who was with him when he died? Was he depressed? Was he really dead or was his death a hoax, an elaborate disappearing act to avoid the public scrutinizing his decline? National and international media converged on Memphis to find out the real story.

Immediately, an advance contingent of the *National Enquirer* team flew by private jet to Memphis. Eventually, the *Enquirer* assigned more than forty editors, staff reporters, private detectives, freelancers,

ELVIS: WHAT HAPPENED

THE
Star 35¢
The American Women's Weekly   Sept. 6, 1977

Read the book
the world is
talking about

Behind the
White House
marriage
bust-up

Guide to
the new
TV shows

Doctors
set to
cure
colds

PRISCILLA
She was
his only
true
love

ELVIS
COLOR
PHOTO
SOUVENIR

Biorhythms
foretold the
fateful story

HOROSCOPE
CALENDAR
FOR SEPTEMBER

"Elvis: What Happened" *Star*™ September 6, 1977.

photographers, rewriters, and researchers to the story. Tom Kuncl, the lead articles editor, arrived in Memphis with fifty thousand dollars earmarked for information and exclusives. When the money reached a low point, the home office sent an additional fifty thousand dollars. The hopeful recipients lined the hallway of the top floor of a hotel reserved for the *Enquirer*. "The only place I could interview witnesses in peace was the bathroom," said Kuncl. Elvis' psychic advisor revealed his communication with his deceased mother. His girlfriend described the moment she found him unconscious on the floor, "Girl Elvis Was Going to Marry Tells Her Heart-Breaking Story!" An inside source sold a copy of the toxicology report to the *Enquirer*. But it was the firsthand witnesses—the death-scene ambulance crew—who rated an all-expenses-paid beach vacation to Lantana, safely removed from the competition.

The *Star* sent ten reporters, also with ample money, to Memphis. They followed their own news trail to the Presley crypt in the Forest Hills Midtown Cemetery. After the funeral, three dubious entrepreneurs plotted to steal Elvis' body from the grave and sell it to the highest bidder. They were caught and arrested, and the exclusive jail cell interview belonged to the *Star*. Prompted by the cadaver-for-profit scheme, the Presley family had the body transported from Forest Hills to a family plot behind the swimming pool at Graceland.

Ultimately, the *Enquirer*—having the most money and the longest reach—prevailed: they secured an exclusive of international proportions, "The Last Picture." Bring back a picture of Elvis in his coffin, Pope said. Beat the competition to the last picture, the irrefutable visual proof that Elvis was dead. The Presley family, protective of his body, banned cameras from the public viewing and hired armed guards to enforce their edict. "It was crazy," said a *Star* reporter. "Reporters were camped out at the gate to Graceland, handing out throwaway cameras to every family member they could bribe."

True to their word, the *Enquirer* never revealed their source, except to admit he was a distant Presley relative. Coached by staff photog-

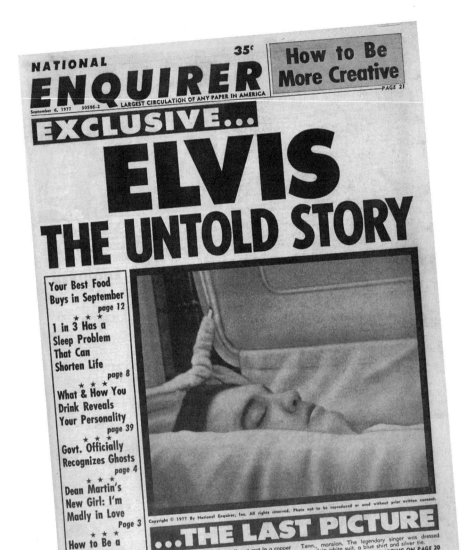

"Elvis The Untold Story" *National Enquirer*™ September 6, 1977.

rapher Jimmy Sutherland, the tabloid recruit slipped into the music room after normal viewing hours and took four pictures of Elvis lying in his coffin.

Now the *Enquirer* was in possession of a very valuable photograph, but if the tabloid could not publish it, the photo was worthless. Accordingly, the *Enquirer* took no chances. Accompanied by a security guard, a reporter escorted the film and the opportunistic picture-taker across the Mississippi River to an isolated airport in West Memphis, Arkansas. A private jet waited, its engines running, primed for takeoff to Florida. In Lantana, the chief of police provided security for the *Enquirer* company car as it drove to the office, where the film was handed over directly to photo editor Brian Hitchen. The first photograph showed the face of the amateur photographer. He had pointed the camera lens backwards. The second photograph captured the chandelier above the coffin. The third and fourth photographs showed Elvis in a white suit and white silk tie at repose in a copper coffin, but the photos were badly out of focus and overexposed. Elvis was barely recognizable until the *Enquirer* retoucher, Bob Stevens, performed his magic. Presley's relative returned to Tennessee eighteen thousand dollars the richer, and the original photographs were locked in Pope's safe, a security measure that persisted for decades. "Exclusive . . . Elvis, the Untold Story," paired with "The Last Picture," sold at an all-time-high, record-breaking six and one half million copies.

The Carol Burnett Libel Suit

Pope's answer to the growing competition was increased spending, riskier ventures, and bigger stories. These tactics paid off in Memphis but backfired in Washington, D.C. "Carol Burnett and Henry K. in Row" was not true, and the *National Enquirer* paid for its mistake with a large legal fee, a protracted court settlement, and plenty of ill-will to go around. A four-sentence gossip column item precipitated what would become a five-year legal battle and a ten million dollar libel suit filed by actor Carol Burnett against the *Enquirer*.

The *Enquirer* reported that Carol Burnett had argued with former secretary of state Henry Kissinger and was "boisterous" in a Washington restaurant. Burnett replied that it was a lie, it was defamatory, and she would see the *Enquirer* in court. Burnett, the daughter of alcoholic parents, intended to make the *Enquirer* pay for insinuating she was intoxicated.

Here was where the tabloid modus operandi, "as revealed by an inside source," backfired. The paid-for information was not credible. Although the *Enquirer* issued a public retraction and apology, Burnett did not back down. Pope had entered a new ball game. He was dealing with a celebrity who possessed enough money and determination to fight about an issue important to her.

This was the first libel suit against the *Enquirer* that led to a court case. Typically, public figures protested a salacious tabloid allegation but did not have the heart or energy to actually pursue a libel suit; unlike Carol Burnett, they settled quickly out of court. A celebrity might or might not prove malicious intent and personal suffering, but in the process the lawsuit created double exposure by keeping an unflattering issue in the news. Additionally, prosecutors had to tangle with an experienced tabloid legal team.

In 1981, five years after the dispute began, a California judge ruled that the *Enquirer* had "acted with reckless disregard for the truth." Burnett was awarded $1.6 million—though that amount was later reduced by over half—in general and punitive damages.

Hollywood and the mainstream press cheered, vilified celebrities lined up to file their own lawsuits, and Pope instituted new rules. Reporters replaced pocket-sized notebooks with pocket-sized tape recorders in order to record and play back all interviews. Quotes had to be verified and confirmed by three additional sources. The *Enquirer*'s Research Department gave peace of mind to Pope and headaches to reporters. Further doubt about a vulnerable story prompted a legal team that specialized in First Amendment law to evaluate content and photographs for any hint of libel or invasion of privacy. The hunt was still on to catch an *Enquirer* misstep, but Pope made the quarry more elusive.

A Quiet Revolution

In 1978 a quiet revolution occurred in Tabloid Valley. Pope introduced new blood into the newsroom, a new look for the *National Enquirer*, and a new tabloid at the supermarkets. Pope enlisted one of his most persuasive editors, Haydon Cameron, a native of Australia, to recruit graduates from prestigious American universities. Pope, who had preconceived ideas of how to gather and write stories, advised, "Just remember, no journalism students." Reaching out of the insular tabloid community, he sought fresh ideas from young, eager college students. "Pope wanted any bright spark from anywhere," said reporter Jim McCandlish.

Initially, three recruits, including a classics major from Harvard University, passed the four-week tryout and joined the *Enquirer*, gradually followed by a succession of American graduates looking for an intriguing and unconventional job. The new blood adopted a pragmatic attitude regarding the maligned tabloids. The *Enquirer* was what it was, a tabloid, not the *New York Times*. They relished the opportunity to collect a generous salary, travel, run with a pack of adventuresome Brits, and be part of a successful tabloid experiment. Equally enticing, they could enjoy spring break year-round in Florida.

In another break from tradition, the black-and-white *Enquirer*, a plain Jane compared to the eye-catching, brightly colored pages of the *Star*, updated its image with color newsprint and a red masthead. While the *Star* did not top the *Enquirer's* circulation sales, it was rising with the under-45 audience, who were sold by its lively celebrity stories, flashy photographs, and television ads. The *Enquirer* responded with a national television campaign that produced instant recognition, "Enquiring Minds Want to Know." Sales increased, in spite of the higher cover price to pay for the added costs.

The *Weekly World News*

Color print requires color printing presses, and following the transition, the *National Enquirer*'s black-and-white printing presses sat idle, a situation unacceptable to Pope and thus giving rise to a new supermarket tabloid in 1978. Initially, Pope's idea was to recycle timeless stories of crime, natural disasters, amazing exploits, and medical cures published by the *Enquirer* years earlier. Phil Bunton, hired by Pope to lead the *Weekly World News*, said he planned to fill the tabloid entirely with true stories, some of which might even have appeared in mainstream news magazines like *Time* or *Newsweek*. The first issue's "Bizarre Death Is Tied to JFK Assassination . . . Cops Hush Up Case after Note Found beside 'Man with No Past'" was an actual story about a man found dead in his car with a note beside his body insinuating he was somehow involved in the Kennedy assassination.

A creative group of successive editors—Phil Bunton, Lou Golden, Dick Long, Joe West, and Eddie Clontz—experimented with different approaches until ultimately a collaborative effort by imaginative and witty writers culminated in an exceptionally clever parody of the tabloids. The *Weekly World News* embraced one purpose: to amuse, with no pretense of reality or reasonable truth.

"Plane Missing since 1939 Lands with Skeleton at the Controls" was a perfect fit for the *Weekly World News*, as was "How to Tell if Your Next Door Neighbor is a Space Alien," which outlined a checklist of nearly ubiquitous characteristics. "Scumbag" was too crude for the *Enquirer*, but not for the *News*. A mainstream newspaper in Florida told of an undertaker who sold body parts; the *News* converted the story to "Florida Man Screams from the Grave, My Brain Is Missing." The British read the *News*; the Japanese read the *News*. The provincials and disaffected believed it; the pop culture aficionados idolized it.

In the back of the *Enquirer* newsroom, four or five *Weekly World News* writers concocted their stories without even leaving the office. Story ideas originated from bizarre news items, or were spun out of whole cloth. "Sometimes at the end of the day my face hurt from laughing so much," said Jack Alexander, a former staff writer. Truth was not allowed to impede the creative process. "Don't question yourself out of a good story. You have got to know when to stop asking questions," said Eddie Clontz, an editor who delighted in a screaming headline and a wild story.

Basically, they made up fictitious stories. It was fun for the staff of the *Weekly World News* and their readers. A very loose interpretation of mass levitations by yogis prompted "The China Jump," followed by a "Counter Jump."

Jump! Join the *Weekly World News* to save the world! We heard, wrote the *News*, that the millions comprising the entire population of China plan to jump up and down in unison. Would the earth be knocked off its orbit? Would it collapse? Would we all go up in flames? Not if there was an intervention, the tabloid hypothesized, a Counter Jump.

The preparations and the hype began. The more bodies and therefore mass behind the jumps, the more effective it would be. The countdown was broadcast from a bar in Queens, New York, a fire department in Massachusetts, a radio station in Wisconsin, a volleyball club in California, and a college dormitory in Texas. At exactly 6 p.m. eastern standard time everyone in the bar, on the beach, in the fire house, and in the dormitory jumped up and down. Nothing happened. Clearly, posited the *News*, the world was saved because the Counter Jump had worked.

In 2000 the *Weekly World News* revisited the theme, "The China Jump: 2 Billion Chinese Will Try to Knock Earth out of Orbit—Again. First Three Attempts Foiled by American Counter Jump." This time,

By JACK ALEXANDER
Staff writer

Bull-ropin', bronc-bustin' cowboy Jimmy Dale Struble was buried with his boots on — standing tall in his grave.

The hard-living, bighearted cowpoke hated to take anything lying down, least of all death. He wanted to enter the hereafter on his feet, wearing his favorite cowboy hat.

And his buddies didn't let him down.

In a simple ceremony in a country cemetery, Jimmy was lowered feet first into his grave, so he could meet his Maker standing up — as a cowboy should. "He was a cowboy to the core," said close buddy Eddie McElley. "He was a dying breed. He was loud, boisterous, big-hearted, and the best horse-shoer ever to set foot in this valley."

Jimmy, 49, spent the last seven years of his cow-punching life in a wheel-chair, paralyzed from the neck down. He died of lung problems after spelling out

DIAGRAM shows ho is buried — standin his burial wishes to H His paralysis stemm broken neck suffered in 1986 in Hanksvi

Save your troubled marriage — in just 12 minutes

It takes only 12 magic minutes a day to restore vitality to your marriage!

"There are four major turning points in the day. If you and your spouse can enjoy three minutes together at these four intervals, you can improve almost any relationship," declares top psychiatrist Dr. Berthold Schwarz.

Dr. Schwarz outlined the four times:

AWAKENING — "The first three minutes of the day should be a comforting time for you both. If you can start off on a positive foot, the rest of the day will be vastly improved. You can smile, give each other a little squeeze or hug, help with the kids or let the dog out. More romantic types can go as far as saying, 'I love you.'"

PARTING — "It's smart to part on a helpful, uplifting note so that you remember

each other this way through-out the day. The wife should look presentable even if she isn't going to work — brush her hair and teeth, put on an attractive robe. The husband can give her a kiss and offer to pick up anything she might need for dinner."

RETURNING — "Set the stage for a lovely evening together by making the return of the husband a peaceful, soothing time. Give each other a few minutes to unwind. Tell each other about something good or humorous that happened."

BEDTIME — "This is the time to ease out of any problems or arguments that occurred during the day. Try to make up if you've had a fight or at least arrive at a neutral ground so you can both get a good night's sleep."

Dr. Schwarz cautioned: "Be positive and mean what you say. If you don't mean it, it won't do much good."

Giant moth smells WORSE

Scientists have discovered a new species of monster moth that releases a stench so horrendous that it is more than twice as powerful as skunk stink!

The unidentified moth, discovered in Chile, South Ameri-

ca, has a 2-foot wing has been known to anyone within 10 when it lets loose its odors, say experts.

WEEKLY WORLD NEWS February 9 1993

however, "The China Jump" did not connect with its readers; it was a new era with different views regarding entertainment.

Writers gathered information as if their stories were real, and got a kick out of illustrating them with recycled photographs of staff writers and their relatives which had been modified to show them in different guises, states of decrepitude or youth, and locations. The trick was to fool readers by lending the stories a degree of plausibility, accomplished by throwing in scientific facts, authentic background details, and an appropriate cast of characters.

COURAGEOUS to the core! Crippled bronc-buster Jimmy Struble's dying wish was to be buried with his boots on — and his body standing up!

Crippled cowpoke wanted to WALK into Heaven!

and another guy it out over who was r roper. y owned a bulldog Buster. When Jimmy Buster got mad," said on" Burns. "Buster the other guy's dog ell broke loose. y was thumpin' the y real good when the ddy picked up a base- and bashed Jimmy on , breaking his neck. d him like a brother," ns, who took care of ter his paralysis. "But ould get a bellyful of out five minutes. Jim- an off-the-wall individ- n there was nothing e said, Jimmy would

loved country music a rough life trapping he and drinking beer r met a horse or bull 't ride when the beer came better get the hell out if you couldn't stand " Glenn Younger said. like as not, there was some fightin' ' ds say Jimmy made mise not to bury him wn. "He hated sitting ais butt for seven buried that way," unger. was used to roping breaking and shoe- rses, hunting bear pping coyotes was a hard-headed y boy — make that on the country boy." eral dozen of Jim- riends, neighbors,

his two broth- ers, two daughters and oth- er family members waded through boot-top-high snow to carry out the crippled cow- puncher's last wishes.

Before they closed the coffin, Jimmy's broth- er, Clifford, put a pocket knife in the deceased man's hand, "In case he wants out of there, he's going to need a good knife," he said.

Jimmy's sad- dle-draped cas- ket was loaded into the back end of his best friend's pickup truck and driv- en down the road to Glade Park Cemetery in Grand Junc- tion, Colo. A friend sang and strummed the last yippee-yi- ya, yippee-yi-yo of *Ghost Rid- ers in the Sky* as tough-talking cowboys pushed their hats low- er on their foreheads — to hide the tears in their eyes. Then they looped their lariats around his coffin and lowered it verti- cally into the grave.

Angry 5-year-old shoots his parents

A 5-year-old tot grabbed his dad's shotgun and blew his parents away — because they didn't get him anything for Christ- mas.

Cops were called to the

... after naughty boy got nothing for Christmas!

youngster's home after neigh- bors saw him sitting on the front steps of the family's home in Melbourne, Australia

— with the gun at his feet. "He was upset when his dad and mom said he wasn't getting anything for Christmas be-

cause he'd been bad," said a detective. "He pouted for an hour or so, then shot them as they watched TV."

35

"Cowboy's Corpse Buried—Standing Up" *Weekly World News*™ February 9, 1993.

If a kernel of a story was extracted from an actual news event, it was embellished with a tabloid twist. Certainly, cowpoke Jimmy Dale Struble from Grand Junction, Colorado, would have been delighted to know that his dying wish earned him a lead role in a *Weekly World News* story, "Cowboy's Corpse Buried—Standing Up!"

A small obituary notice in a Colorado newspaper noted that Jimmy Dale Struble, paralyzed from the neck down when he suffered a bro- ken neck during a bar fight, was buried standing up in a vertically positioned coffin. The obituary was real. "He didn't want to crawl into

Heaven" was pure writer's inspiration. Staff writer Jack Alexander set the stage with an actual head shot of Struble, a "hard headed country boy," introduced as "Courageous to the Core . . . Crippled Bronco Buster Jimmy Struble's Dying Wish Was to be Buried with his Boots On . . . and His Body Standing Up." A sketch showed how the cowboy was buried standing up in his coffin. The text was peppered with quotes that perfectly blended folksy commentary and humor. "I loved him like a brother," said best buddy Dan Boon Burns, "but even I could get a bellyful of him in 5 minutes. When there was nothing left to be said, Jimmy would say it." Clifford, Struble's brother, placed a pocketknife in the casket, "in case he wants out of there he's going to need a good knife." As the upright coffin was lowered into the ground, guitar strains of "yippie-yi-o-ki-yay" drifted over Clark Cemetery.

Globe Communications

By the beginning of the 1980s the *National Enquirer* and the *Weekly World News*, owned by Generoso Pope Jr., and the *Star*, owned by Rupert Murdoch, were solidly established in the national supermarkets as viable tabloids. "My real goal is worldwide circulation, second to none," said Pope. Pope never achieved his goal of an international customer base twenty million strong, one capable of influencing world affairs, but the mass appeal of his successful tabloid formula was too fruitful to be ignored by other entrepreneurs.

Michael Rosenbloom, a successful Canadian businessman with a background in finance, founded Globe Communications in 1970 when he bought two Canadian tabloids: a financially strapped and notorious *Midnight*, and an unremarkable *National Examiner*. Rosenbloom set his sights on the American supermarket trade, which he penetrated by embracing supermarket-acceptable content and distributing his product through supermarket outlets. He recruited two experts from the *Enquirer*, one a marketing executive with influential contacts, and the other an editor, Selig Adler, who deftly eliminated graphically sexual and violent content from the story mix.

The *Midnight* changed first to the *Midnight Globe* and then to just the *Globe*. The *Globe* and the *National Examiner* copied the supermarket tabloid formula of mixing celebrity gossip, advice columns, and human interest stories. The *Globe* set a deliberately off-center tone, "Cheers Star's Father is Named JFK Killer." The *Examiner* went with "Quick—What's Brown & Sounds like Big Ben? Dungggg!" a story of clocks made from cow dung. Incredible, said the readers, and they bought the tabloid.

Murdoch was content to remain in the metropolitan New York City area, but Rosenbloom had apparently reached his saturation point of Canadian winters and strident work unions. He relocated Globe Communications to West Palm Beach and moved again in 1982 to Boca Raton, seventeen miles south of Lantana. Like Pope, Rosen-

Rat's Mouth or Thieves' Inlet?

Boca Raton, translated literally from Spanish, means "rat's mouth." But if you are one of Boca Raton's glamorous citizens, you might not want to be associated with a rat's mouth. The alternative, hotly debated translations are "hidden rocks inlet," "thieves' inlet," and "the mouth of the Ratone River." Or there is "Boca," the nickname of a chic affluent city by the sea with eighty thousand inhabitants.

In 1982 Boca Raton offered everything that Generoso Pope Jr. avoided in Lantana—upscale restaurants and shopping, art museums, movie theaters, dance clubs, golf courses, and polo fields. Oceanfront condos and penthouses sold for millions of dollars. Boca was pink stucco walls, terra cotta tile roofs, and black wrought iron gates, the heritage of the 1920s society architect Addison Mizner. It was, and still is, a subtropical playground and a corporate center.

bloom was attracted to the Gold Coast of Florida by its sunshine, low taxes, and non-union employees. He inherited an additional resource, though: a reservoir of talented and experienced tabloid editors and reporters. Friday afternoon, Pope fired; Monday morning, Rosenbloom hired.

In 1982 Rosenbloom built a contemporary three-story office building in an attractively landscaped Boca Raton business park to house his tabloid conglomerate, Globe Communications. At the entrance to the Globe offices, a larger-than-life bronzed sculpture of the mythological god Atlas grasped a globe of the world.

For several years the *Weekly World News* cornered the market for outlandish stories, but in 1983 Globe Communications introduced a third tabloid, the *Sun*, edited by John Vader, cofounder of *Midnight*. Modeled after the *News*, the *Sun*, printed in full color to stand apart from the black-and-white *News*, was perfectly capable of inventing its own crazy stories, "Woman Turns into Wild Dog . . . after Being Forced to Eat Pet Food for 3 Yrs."

Although hemmed in by three weekly tabloids in Boca Raton and one in New York City, Pope retained his position as leader of the largest-selling and wealthiest of the supermarket tabloids, but he no longer monopolized tabloid readers' attentions or wallets. Each week Pope received instant feedback from his readers. Thursday, the latest issue of the *Enquirer* appeared in the supermarkets; by Monday, Pope knew if circulation had increased or decreased. By the mid-1980s he noticed that the market and the readers' tastes were changing. "I Killed John Belushi" sold more papers than "Mother of First 'Nobel' Sperm Bank Baby Tells Her Own Story." Consequently, the *Enquirer*'s original editorial formulation shifted to overwhelmingly favor celebrity stories. The celebrity could be a movie star, a criminal, or a politician; the only proviso was that they be high-profile and their activities command attention.

John Belushi

When the *National Enquirer* concentrated their investigative skills on a current news event instead of Bigfoot, it produced exclusives with a national impact. In 1982 the reporting team of Larry Haley and Tony Brenna received the J. Edgar Hoover Memorial Gold Medal Award for Distinguished Public Service in the investigation of John Belushi's death. The honor, usually reserved for a police officer, is awarded each year by the American Police Hall of Fame, a national organization of United States police chiefs.

On March 5, 1982, actor John Belushi died in Southern California from a suspected overdose of cocaine and heroin. The Los Angeles Police Department questioned and released the last person assumed to have seen Belushi alive, an alleged drug dealer referred to as the "mystery woman." This was exactly the type of information that tantalized the *Enquirer*. Haley wanted to know, "Who was she and why did the police let her go?"

The "mystery woman" was Cathy Smith, known as "Cathy Silverbag," described by the *Enquirer* as a courier who "carried her deadly goodies in a silver purse." After the police released her, she fled to Toronto, Canada.

Haley and Brenna acted on what was potentially an important story. It was not clear what story Smith had to sell or what she would be willing to tell, but they tracked her down in Toronto and negotiated an interview. Over a period of ten days the reporters taped a twenty-hour, detailed account of Smith's role in Belushi's death. In a spectacularly candid admission, she disclosed that she supplied heroin to Belushi and personally administered some of the approximately twenty-four heroin-cocaine "speedball" injections he took in his final thirty hours. "I Killed John Belushi. I didn't mean to—but I was responsible for his death . . . I wish it had been me who died. It should have been me!" sobbed Cathy Smith to the *Enquirer*.

Her story created "a media explosion." Over a period of several weeks, network evening news broadcasts and news magazines repeated again and again the details of Smith's confession. In an unusual recognition by mainstream media, tabloid reporters Haley and Brenna were cited by name as the investigative reporters who broke the case.

Although the investigative efforts of the *Enquirer* crucially impacted a murder case receiving national attention, circulation sales for the exclusive were less than extraordinary. By the end of the week of the breaking story, the mainstream media was vigorously pursuing it, but the next issue of the *Enquirer* appeared on the supermarket racks with new stories, and the readers moved on.

As a result of the *Enquirer*'s thoroughly researched and documented confessional story, the California State Attorney's Office reopened the case, and the tapes were subpoenaed and verified as authentic. A tedious extradition from Canada to California, the prosecuting state, dragged on from 1982 to 1985. The reporters testified twice as key witnesses before a grand jury. Ultimately, Smith pled guilty to involuntary manslaughter and was sentenced to a prison term.

Gary Hart

The mission of the *National Enquirer* in the 1980s was business as usual; uncover the story that the competition overlooked and get the exclusive. The mission of the competition was to thwart the *Enquirer*. Fueled by the challenge, the *Enquirer* accelerated its pace to expose more and greater celebrity secrets. In 1987, Senator Gary Hart chose an inauspicious time to test the *Enquirer*'s determination.

"Follow me around. I don't care," said presidential candidate Gary Hart in a *New York Times* interview when questioned about a rumor of infidelity. "I'm serious. If anybody wants to put a tail on me, go ahead. They'd be very bored." But he was mistaken: a politician suspected of an extramarital affair and deceit is anything but boring.

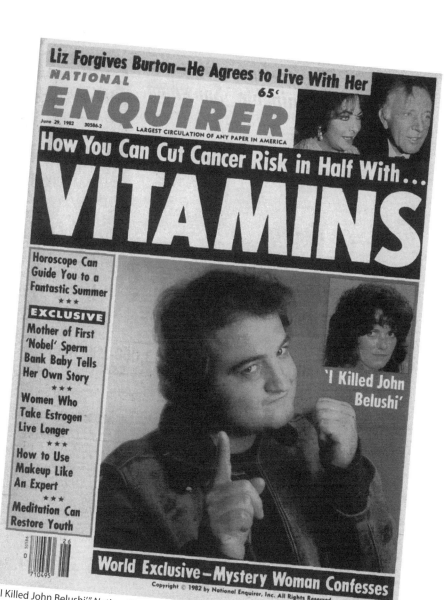

"'I Killed John Belushi'" *National Enquirer*™ June 29, 1982.

Though the unnamed tipster for the scandal contacted the mainstream *Miami Herald*, they put the *Enquirer* onto the trail nonetheless. "Gary Hart is having an affair with a friend of mine," said the source. Acting on the anonymous phone call, three *Herald* reporters, Jim McGee, Tom Fiedler, and James Savage, traveled to Georgetown, D.C., to stake out Hart's townhouse—the site where he was reported to have planned a rendezvous with Donna Rice, the informant's friend. The *Herald* reporters verified Hart was at the townhouse, as was his female friend, but did she spend the night? There the story remained in limbo, ready to be picked up by the *Enquirer*.

Larry Haley, the story editor, sent a lead sheet to Pope that read, "Let's probe for our own angle on Gary Hart." Haley admitted, "We didn't have the foggiest idea where it would land us. It was a massive fishing expedition." But the *Enquirer* had enough manpower and confidence to follow any lead that interested Pope, no matter how obscure.

Senior reporter Alan Smith uncovered in Los Angeles the critical piece of information that there existed photographs of Rice and Hart aboard the yacht "Monkey Business," in the midst of a sailing cruise that took them from Miami to Bimini in the Bahamas. One was a particularly entertaining and incriminating photo of Hart, who was wearing a T-shirt with "Monkey Business Crew" emblazoned across it and holding mini-skirted Rice on his lap. Immediately, reporters Richard Baker and John South, soon to be reinforced by additional staff, drove from Lantana to Miami.

While the *Enquirer* team canvassed Miami to locate the owner of the photograph, one *Star* reporter happened to be in Miami covering a story on dying actor Jackie Gleason. Celebrity illness sells tabloids, though not as well as a sex scandal. It is likely that the *Star* and *Enquirer* reporters crossed paths at one of the bars frequented by journalists, but no one at the *Star* or in the rest of the media had a clue that the "Monkey Business" photographs existed until the *Enquirer* published them.

Donna Rice — What Really Happened

NATIONAL ENQUIRER

65¢

June 2, 1987   30586-2

LARGEST CIRCULATION OF ANY PAPER IN AMERIC

GARY HART ASKED ME TO MARRY HIM

Exclusive Photos of Fun-Filled Weekend in the Bahamas

Vanna to Wed Linda Evans' Ex-Fiance

How Paul Newman Played Cupid for Tom Cruise & Bride

"Donna Rice—What Really Happened: Gary Hart Asked Me to Marry Him" *National Enquirer™* June 2, 1987.

It was not a simple process for the *Enquirer* to acquire the photographs and attain the exclusive rights to them. The *Enquirer* had to locate the person who owned the photographs, verify their authenticity, negotiate a contract, and keep the competition at bay. It had to act quickly but with secrecy. It accomplished the mission in two weeks, from the afternoon that the *Enquirer* reporters rushed to Miami to the morning when photo editor John Cathcart drove back to Lantana with the photographs in his possession.

"Exclusive Photos of Fun-Filled Weekend in the Bahamas" completed the story begun by the *Miami Herald*. The story created doubt about Hart's credibility as a presidential candidate, and disgraced, he withdrew his candidacy. The photographs were the envy of every newspaper and magazine and clearly exhibited the power of the *National Enquirer*. This was a huge coup and forced the rest of the media to take note of how the *Enquirer* had unleashed its forces upon political celebrities.

Apparently, politicians did not take note. Twenty years later, in 2007, former North Carolina senator John Edwards, a contender for the Democratic presidential candidacy, was similarly brought into the spotlight by the *Enquirer*. The breaking story claimed he was having an extramarital affair with Riele Hunter, and included a photograph of her, obviously pregnant. Edwards dismissed the story as "tabloid trash." Eight months later, however, after continual denials, Edwards finally admitted to having the extramarital affair and faced the potential political fallout that entailed. Once again, the *Enquirer* received begrudging credit from major news organizations for its investigative journalism.

Within Tabloid Valley, the competition was predictable; the tabloids chased celebrities mercilessly and yet there still seemed to be enough celebrity news to go around. Pope watched Murdoch and Rosenbloom; Murdoch and Rosenbloom watched Pope. It was the competition outside the Tabloid Valley group that surprised the decision-makers of the supermarket tabloids. By the end of the 1980s,

A Pope Commendation

When a reporter or editor produced an excellent story, Generoso Pope Jr. acknowledged their accomplishment. On June 4, 1987, he sent a letter of commendation to Larry Haley for "your outstanding contributions to our Gary Hart scoop." He went on to say, "I am truly grateful for your efforts in helping us quickly complete this top-priority assignment. Please accept my sincere thanks for the superb job you did. In recognition of your hard work and unselfish dedication, I am enclosing a well-deserved bonus check for you."

GP Group, Inc.

600 South East Coast Avenue
Lantana, Florida 33462 · 305-586-1111

June 4, 1987

Mr. Larry Haley
432 Palmetto Drive
Lake Park, FL 33403

Dear Larry:

I would like to take this opportunity to express my personal appreciation for your outstanding contributions to our Gary Hart scoop. I am truly grateful for your efforts in helping us to quickly complete this top-priority assignment.

Please accept my sincere thanks for the superb job you did. In recognition of your hard work and unselfish dedication, I am enclosing a well-deserved bonus check for you.

Again, my thanks for the excellent job you did.

Sincerely,

Generoso Pope Jr.
Chairman

GP:sn

Enclosure

Distribution Services, Inc. • Fairview Printing, Inc. • Fairview Real Estate, Inc. • National Distribution Services, Inc.
National Enquirer, Inc. • Weekly World News, Inc.

Letter from Generoso Pope Jr. to Larry Haley, courtesy of Larry Haley.

celebrity news—traditionally the domain of tabloids—became a popular component of the expanded mainstream media. Scandal and gossip were fascinating and entertaining to potential readers and viewers, the mainstream media had learned.

Murdoch reacted to the competition by expanding into tabloid television with his Fox production, *A Current Affair*. *Time Inc.* responded with a weekly celebrity magazine, *People*, designed "to do serious journalism about famous people, even if it involved frivolous subjects."

Pope was next in line for a bold move. Would he challenge Murdoch in the cable television industry? Would he reshape the supermarket tabloid? Unfortunately, Pope did not have an opportunity to respond to the changing market conditions. On October 2, 1988, he died of a heart attack.

Chapter 6

Post-Pope

"I WOULD LIKE for them to say I made an awful lot of people happy and gave them relief and escape. Millions and millions of them," said Generoso Pope Jr. On Sunday morning, October 2, 1988, Pope died of a heart attack at age sixty-one. The *New York Times* wrote, "Generoso P. Pope Jr. Dead at 61; *The National Enquirer*'s Publisher." The *New York Post* preferred, "*National Enquirer* Owner Goes to Meet Elvis."

Monday morning the editorial staff of the *National Enquirer* and the *Weekly World News* returned to work, writing stories about a celebrity wedding, a television sitcom feud, and an alien sighting. It was not quite business as usual—Pope, the boss, was gone—but "the reader comes first."

Pope's death unlocked the potential for quantum change. Who would be Pope's successor? Would the *Enquirer* be sold? Would it lose its first-place position to the *Globe* or the *Star*? What would happen to the world's biggest Christmas party?

The World's Biggest Christmas Party

"Pope was a good corporate citizen," said Michael Bornstein, Lantana town manager. "Anytime the police, fire company, ambulance service needed a new vehicle or equipment, he provided." Pope the philan-thropist contributed to the JFK Medical Center in Atlantis, a local

Christmas tree. (Courtesy of the Town of Lantana.)

Christmas display. (Courtesy of the Town of Lantana.)

orphanage, the Little League baseball team, the high school band, and the Fourth of July firework display. Pope the sentimentalist invited the community and the world to what he proclaimed to be the biggest Christmas party—complete with the tallest Christmas tree—in the world; remember that this was Tabloid Valley.

Each summer Dino Gallo, far more familiar with the sidewalks of New York City than the forests of the Pacific Northwest, tramped through tree farms in Washington and Oregon to select the perfect Christmas tree. It had to be at least 125 five feet tall, though a height of 150 feet was optimal. In order for the tree to fit on a flatbed railroad car, two-thirds of the branches were sawed off and numbered. When the tree arrived in Lantana, a large crane swung it into place on the *Enquirer* lawn. Then the tree was ready for a civic-minded motorcycle club from Tampa to rumble into town and spend a week inserting the branches back into its trunk and decorating it. Fifteen thousand lights adorning the tree cast a glow as far as the Lantana interchange, two miles to the west. A six-foot silver star topped the tree, which was covered with miles of tinsel garland, thousands of colored balls, red bows, and striped candy canes.

Surrounding the tree, fourteen thousand feet of model train track transported miniature trains in and out of alpine villages. Above the landscaped paths of the *Enquirer's* grounds, tiny mechanical flying saucers flew along wires stretched between palm trees and deposited their alien passengers at McSpace Burger, greeted there by a blinking sign reading "UFO's Welcome." Automated cartoon characters, a Christmas crèche, an Elvis impersonator, a host of aliens, Santa's elves, and a volunteer fireman dressed as Santa Claus entertained an estimated twenty-five thousand people a day from ten o'clock in the morning until midnight.

To accommodate the influx of tourists and accordingly clogged streets, Pope hired temporary security guards. Jack Carpenter, a member of the Lantana Historical Society, recalled that he earned almost twice as much per hour as a holiday policeman as he did at his fulltime job working for Pratt & Whitney. "Everything died when Pope died," said Carpenter. Most notably for Lantana, they lost their Christmas CEO. Without Pope to personally spend an estimated one million dollars on the Christmas extravaganza, Lantana was forced to relinquish its status as the home of Christmas in Florida.

American Media Incorporated

The usual options for the transfer of power in a closely-held family business, especially one operated, inspired, and energized by a sole proprietor, are either to select a successor from within the family or sell the company to an outside party. Pope handed the power of decision regarding his estate to three trustees. Within three months, Pope's tabloid holdings, the *National Enquirer* and the *Weekly World News*, were for sale. Elvis did not descend from the heavens in a spaceship to buy the *Enquirer*, as suggested by a *Palm Beach Post* cartoon, but plenty of other interested parties submitted their proposals. "Whoever buys the *Enquirer* and the *Weekly World News* is really buying their hold on tabloid supermarket exposure," commented the *Wall Street Journal*.

Six months after Pope died, MacFadden Holdings Inc., publisher of *True Story* and *True Confessions*, and Boston Ventures, a venture capital investment group, paid more than four hundred million dollars for the *National Enquirer* and the *Weekly World News*. Less than a year later the new owners offered nearly the same daunting figure for purchase of the *Star*. At the time Murdoch was in the process of expanding his North American media interests beyond a weekly tabloid. He sold the *Star*, but retained his daily tabloid, the *New York Post*, as part of his world conglomerate, News Corporation.

Peter Callahan, Michael Boylan, and Mannie Rabinowitz orchestrated the buying spree at MacFadden Holdings Inc. "The three suits," as they were called by the Brits, led the *National Enquirer*, the *Weekly World News*, and the *Star* into the corporate world as one entity, American Media Incorporated (AMI).

Lantana missed its benefactor Generoso Pope Jr., but the residents were relieved; the *Enquirer* and the *News* maintained their headquarters in the low-rise brick building on Southeast Coast Avenue. When in town, reporters from the *Star* joined their new colleagues for a toast (though seldom limited to one) at the Whistle Stop or the Hawaiian Ocean Inn, but the *Star* remained based in its news office in Tarrytown, New York.

For Pope the *Enquirer* was his first-born, his most prized personal possession. He poured money extravagantly into it and controlled the editorial decisions, accountable only to himself. While the new corporate owners conscientiously maintained the flavor of the Lantana weeklies, the tabloid conglomerate of AMI was a business enterprise, and was accountable to its investors. Reporters continued to travel to distant assignments, but expense accounts were more carefully regulated. The community Christmas party was eliminated, but the staff Christmas party was lavish.

Sixty employees were laid off, television advertising was reduced, and the price of the *Enquirer* increased from seventy-five cents for sixty-four pages to eighty-five cents for fifty-six pages. The *Enquirer's* unique system of rival editorial teams, each swollen with extra expenses and manpower for the sake of better competition, was replaced with the traditional organizational pattern of several editors sharing reporters and resources. Released from Pope's restrictions, reporters reverted from taping everything to taking traditional notes, thereby speeding up the production process.

Salaries and funds for confidential sources and exclusives continued to be higher than the industry average and that pleased the employees. Reduced spending and efficient management practices maximized profits and that pleased the investors. Although increased competition from celebrity magazines, cable television, and the Internet precipitated a decline in circulation sales, four years after the acquisition AMI reported a profit of $120 million.

Who Gets the Scoop?

The *National Enquirer*, as the better-selling of the *Enquirer/Star* celebrity pair, retained its pre-AMI status quo with abundant resources and staff. "The *Star*," said former editor-in-chief Richard Kaplan, "had to be more aggressive to compete with less resources."

Frequently the *Star* and the *Enquirer* learned of and pursued a celebrity rumor concurrently. Although the reporters received their paychecks from the same source, they still competed with one another as before the merger. "At the reporting level we considered our fellow reporters rivals," said former *Star* reporter Steven Edwards. "The reporter's job is to beat the opposition, so people from the *Star* tried to beat reporters on the *National Enquirer*, and vice versa. At the executive management level, there appeared to be collusion to the extent that the two publications usually didn't have the same story played big as lead on both covers. To my knowledge, there was never any sharing of content."

Which tabloid won the front page lead? The decision really depended upon who was first on the scene, developed the most interesting angle, or obtained an important photograph or exclusive interview. When the *Star* beat the *Enquirer* to an exclusive story by a narrow margin, it earned the cover story and photograph. Consequently, the lead story in the *Star* might appear as a "down-story" in a small box at the bottom of the front page on the *Enquirer*.

Together the two AMI celebrity tabloids and the *Weekly World News* dominated the Tabloid Valley weeklies in sales and exclusives, but south of Lantana in Boca Raton, at the corporate headquarters of Globe Communications, Michael Rosenbloom changed tactics to position the *Globe* as a serious contender for celebrity exclusives.

When the *Globe* joined the supermarket tabloid community in 1982, it was not considered a great threat by the *Star* or the *National Enquirer*. Absent from the scene of breaking news, the *Globe* splashed headlines frequently based on recycled rumors across its front pages. To raise the *Globe*'s status and increase its sales, Rosenbloom hired Phil Bunton, a former Fleet Streeter who was instrumental in molding the *Star* when it was founded by Rupert Murdoch in New York City. Bunton recruited aggressive reporters and experienced writers, many of them from the competition in Lantana. For improved credibility and protection against libel, he instituted a new fact-checking system. Reporters were supplied with expense accounts to chase a breaking story and funds to compete for confidential information. In 1991 an energized *Globe* debuted with a controversial exposé.

The Kennedy Smith Debate

"Should This Woman Be Named?" asked journalist Margaret Carlson in *Time* magazine. The London *Sunday Mirror* newspaper thought she should, and they identified by name the woman who accused William Kennedy Smith of sexual assault at the Kennedy family estate in Palm Beach. But that was in England; in the United States, journalists traditionally abide by a professional code that dictates they withhold the name of the victim of an alleged sex crime. The *Globe*, however, overcame this initial restraint, "Kennedy Rape Gal Exposed." Ethics disregarded, it went for the scoop.

The day after the *Globe* published the alleged victim's name and a high school photograph of her, NBC *Nightly News* broadcast the *Globe*'s indiscretion. In reporting about the *Globe*'s story, though, NBC became the second American media outlet to name the victim. As a matter of public information, the *New York Times* followed suit, but it incurred vociferous criticism from its readers for disclosing her name, especially in an unsympathetic tabloid-style story that described the victim's speeding tickets, high school grades, and love affairs. Everyone wanted a piece of the tabloid story that involved such a famous political family as the Kennedys.

Which should triumph: the public's right to know or the victim's right to privacy? Once the identity of the reputed victim is legitimately obtained from public court records, the information is legally available to the public. The *Globe* repeated information that had been previously published, what was common knowledge among reporters camped outside the Kennedy estate and the home of the accuser. It was only a matter of time, the *Globe* reasoned, before someone in the media leaked the woman's identity.

Some believed that withholding the name of an alleged rape victim implied undeserved shame; others argued that publishing the name exposed the victim to undeserved public humiliation. Although the majority of news organizations refrained from publishing the woman's name, the debate became a moot point when the trial was televised live from the courtroom in Palm Beach. A blue blob protected the woman's face from view on the television screen, but the sordid details of the trial were revealed live to millions of viewers. "It's Dallas.

> ## The State of Florida v. Globe Communications
>
> The State of Florida attempted to prosecute Globe Communications for their indiscretion in the Kennedy Smith case by citing a state statute that prohibited a Florida-based publisher from naming the victims of sex crimes. A local county court judge ruled that the First Amendment guarantees freedom of the press to report matters of public interest, and in this case, the victim's identity became public record when she filed a police report and initiated a court trial. The case was appealed in 1994 before the Florida Supreme Court, and the decision was upheld in a ruling that continues to be significant in media law. The *Globe* was satisfied; it achieved its exclusive and sold many papers.

It's Perry Mason. It's Rashomon," wrote journalist Walter Goodman in the *New York Times*.

The *National Enquirer* waited for their exclusive. "Our hope is that we can get her to sell her story to us and take the onus off us," said executive editor Dan Schwartz in an interview with the *Palm Beach Post*. But after Kennedy Smith was acquitted, his accuser upstaged the tabloids. She told her story without the benefit of checkbook journalism to Diane Sawyer on ABC's *Prime Time Live*. The interview generated what were *Prime Time Live*'s highest ratings at the time, and captured a larger audience than its competition, *L.A. Law* and *Knots Landing*.

Gennifer Flowers

The *Globe* stepped boldly to be the first to name the victim of Kennedy Smith's alleged sexual assault. In 1992 the *Star* moved swiftly and skillfully to investigate the rumor of a presidential candidate's extramarital affairs.

After a brief hiatus, in 1992 the *Star* was "back to the business of hard tabloid style journalism," said former editor-in-chief Dick Kaplan. In 1985, Rupert Murdoch experimented with a new image for the *Star*. A sleazy tabloid did not attract influential national advertisers; a magazine-style tabloid that cloaked celebrity gossip in a softer tone and attracted women readers with fluffy lifestyle articles was more what they were looking for. Murdoch sought a savvy editor, an American experienced in magazine journalism. Without a doubt, Kaplan fit the bill. He had earned a journalism degree from the Columbia University School of Journalism and had served as executive editor of the *Ladies Home Journal* and *US Weekly*.

The milder-mannered *Star* attracted advertising revenue from Proctor & Gamble, General Foods, Philip Morris, and Lever Bros., but in the supermarket the celebrity gossip devotees preferred the sensational headlines of the *National Enquirer* and the *Globe*. When circulation sales hit a plateau and did not overtake the competition, the *Star* reverted to "a juicy celebrity-journalism publication."

A politician was not the usual celebrity target of the *Star*, but speculations about a presidential candidate's sex life promised to be amply juicy. In 1992 an article in the *Wall Street Journal* hinted at reports of Democratic presidential candidate Bill Clinton's alleged infidelities during his terms as governor of Arkansas. It was just a rumor for the mainstream press. It was pay dirt for the *Star*.

"Dig," Kaplan told his staff at the Monday morning story meeting. For the remainder of the morning, Marion Collins, a native Scottish reporter, was on the phone gathering information. Before noon she uncovered an ignored lawsuit filed by dismissed Clinton employee Larry Nichols that claimed Governor Clinton spent public money on extramarital relationships with five women. By that afternoon, the *Star*'s Arkansas freelancer Chris Bell was in Little Rock searching through the files at the courthouse. Next morning, a copy of the thirty-page lawsuit was lying on Kaplan's desk, and an hour later, *Star* reporter and Brit Steven Edwards was on his way from Tarrytown, New York, to Little Rock, Arkansas.

The *Star* was not the only publication that read the *Wall Street Journal*. Among others, the *Washington Post* was on Clinton's trail. Edwards needed to be efficient, resourceful, and accurate.

Edwards began his investigation with the plaintiff, Larry Nichols. "There are three possible motives driving a person to inform on another: civic duty, money and revenge. Journalists prefer sources who open up out of a sense of civic duty. Such sources are less likely to exaggerate or twist the story," said Edwards in "Bill Clinton, Gennifer Flowers, and Me." Nichols did not demand a lot of money, but he was disgruntled enough about his job dismissal to talk. Based on background information provided by Nichols, Edwards tackled the accusations by tracking down the five women named in the lawsuit.

Only one of the five women, Gennifer Flowers, confirmed Nichols's accusation and agreed to meet with Edwards. An angry, scorned Flowers told *Star* readers, "I'm so tired of all the lying and hiding. For 12 years I was his girlfriend, and now he tells me to deny it—to say it isn't true." Clinton, wrote the *Star*, said the allegations were "trash, old news—an absolute, total lie . . . the *Star* says Martians walk on the earth and people have cows' heads." Kaplan replied to this comment in a *Time* magazine interview, "This isn't Martians walking the earth. This is a very, very real inquiry into the integrity of a major presidential candidate."

Initially, Flowers wanted to tell her story to the *Washington Post*, a mainstream newspaper. When she realized, however, that the *Star* offered high-profile publicity, a huge and sympathetic audience, and payment for exclusive rights to her story, she opted for the *Star*.

Typically, signing an exclusive contract with the tabloids involves a negotiating process conducted with secrecy and urgency. Understandably, Flowers was reluctant to reveal her information prior to payment, and the *Star* did not want to pay her until it verified that the information was accurate and, most importantly, that the tapes were authentic. An interim contract stipulated that Flowers would agree to reveal her information, but the *Star* would not publish it until confirmed, and a final fixed fee contingent upon confirmation and reputed to be six figures was negotiated. The *Star* applied its usual standards to support the validity of the exposé—the tapes were evaluated to assess their implications of an intimate relationship, they were verified as undoctored, and Flowers passed a lie detector test. Reportedly, her story was also backed up by two additional sources, a friend and her mother.

On January 28, 1992, the *Star* published the allegations of Nichols's lawsuit, "Dem's Front-Runner Bill Clinton Cheated with Miss America and Four Other Beauties—a Former Miss Arkansas, a Singer, a Reporter and His Own Press Spokeswoman." A week later on February 4th, the second installment of "Sex Scandal Rocks Race for White

"Feed the Press"

The Flowers story, in terms of national publicity more significant for the *Star* than entertaining gossip, deserved a release party. The national media was invited to a public relations event at the Waldorf-Astoria Hotel in Manhattan described by the *Washington Post* as "feed the press—a shouting, surging news conference." A giant blowup of the *Star* cover with head shots of Governor Clinton and Gennifer Flowers loomed in back of the *Star's* entourage of AMI executives, editors, reporters, photographers, and Flowers herself, who was accompanied by her attorney. Flowers read from a printed statement, "The truth is I loved him, now he tells me to deny it." The *Star* praised its investigation, but the media was most interested in finding out how much Flowers was paid, if she met with Clinton in the men's room of the Arkansas Governor's Mansion, and if the sex was good.

"My 12-Year Affair With Bill Clinton" *Star*™ February 4, 1992.

House" published Gennifer Flowers's story, "My 12-Year Affair with Bill Clinton Plus the Secret Love Tapes that Prove It!" The third issue on February 11th told "How Bill Got Me My State Job" and printed selected excerpts from the taped telephone conversations, "Tapes—Now You Be the Judge." The *Star* intended to keep the scandal spinning with backup allegations from additional sources. Surely, others motivated by revenge, civic duty, or money would tell it all to the *Star*, but the story ended with Flowers.

"The *Star* was the first news organization to go wide and big about Clinton's womanizing," said Edwards. Although the mainstream media publicized the exposé, critics accused the press of following a sleazy story obtained by paying for information. But the national impact could not be ignored. Four years before the Flowers story, a photograph of Senator Gary Hart and Donna Rice precipitated Hart's withdrawal from the presidential race. Luckily for Clinton, there was no incriminating "Monkey Business" photograph. Unlike Hart, he immediately addressed the allegations on national television and thereby somewhat defused the situation. He did not leave the presidential race and went on to win the nomination and the presidency.

O. J. Simpson and the Supermarket Tabloids

The supermarket tabloids' style of investigative reporting exposed Senator Gary Hart's dalliance, revealed the name of William Kennedy Smith's accuser, and connected the vague Clinton rumors to Gennifer Flowers. As the tabloids picked their scandals from the hard news of crime and politics, the mainstream media dove into the tabloid brand of emotionally packed human dramas. "And the *Enquirer*'s kind has become the mainstream's kind," wrote *Time* magazine law reporter, Andrea Sachs, in "Mud and the Mainstream."

In particular, two impressive examples of what Sachs calls the "melding of mainstream culture and *Enquirer* culture" occurred in 1994: the mass-media coverage of Tonya Harding's assault on rival

Nancy Kerrigan at the Olympic trials for figure-skating, and six months later, the double homicide of Nicole Brown Simpson and Ronald Goldman. From June 1994 until October 1995 the mainstream media and the tabloids competed for coverage of the same story, investigating who murdered Nicole and Ron, and then publicizing the subsequent murder trial of Nicole's ex-husband, football celebrity O. J. Simpson. We were "all drinking from the same trough," said Steven LeGrice, former *Star* executive editor.

The differences in the coverage of the O. J. Simpson story in the various Tabloid Valley weeklies are interesting. Inhibited by a small budget and staff, the *National Examiner* could not send reporters to the crime scene in Los Angeles. Instead, it phoned its sources, "The Juice Cracks!" The *Weekly World News* wrote a phantom tale, "Nicole's Grave Is Empty!" The big three—the *Star*, the *National Enquirer*, and the *Globe*—spread their resources all across Southern California to compete both with each other and an enormous gathering of national and international media.

Shortly after the double homicide occurred in a Los Angeles suburb on June 12, 1994, four reporters from the *National Enquirer* began staking out Nicole Brown Simpson's house, the crime scene, and four more covered O. J. Simpson's home. "Within a few hours it became clear," said lead editor on the story, David Perel, "O. J. Simpson himself was a suspect. I immediately put eight reporters on the story and we were at O. J.'s house before the coroner arrived."

Two days later in Lantana, Steve Coz, the senior editor, and Perel presented their Page One choice at the weekly story meeting. The Simpson/Goldman homicide rose to the top of the story picks. Although O. J. Simpson was not officially a suspect, the *Enquirer* announced their editorial position with a prophetic headline, "The O. J. Murders."

In Tarrytown, New York, four days after the murder, Dick Kaplan, editor-in-chief of the *Star*, was eating lunch in his office when one of his writers rushed in to tell him to turn on the television. On the

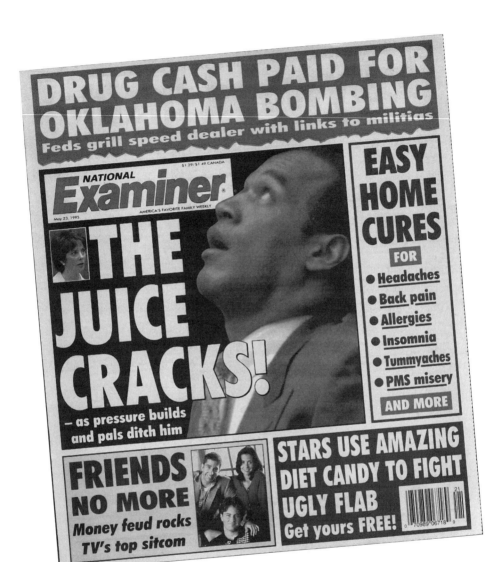

"The Juice Cracks" *National Examiner*™ May 23, 1995.

screen a white Ford Bronco carrying a reportedly suicidal O. J. Simpson, wanted for questioning about the double homicide, led the Los Angeles police on a slow speed chase along Interstate 405. Kaplan ripped up the scheduled cover of the *Star*. Three hours later the *Star* "jammed a big O. J. story onto page one," said Kaplan. "We simply went with what we had—there was no time for deep digging and checkbook journalism that first week. Speed was of the essence."

In Boca Raton at the *Globe* headquarters, editor-in-chief Phil Bunton jumped on the story as the information and photographs flowed in from the *Globe's* frontline reporters in Los Angeles, going for a sensational impact by displaying the autopsy photos of Nicole Brown Simpson. Bunton said, "O. J. was the biggest tabloid story since Elvis died."

Once the three Florida tabloids exhausted the initial details of the active crime scene, they defined their approach according to the changing situation and their readers' interest. The theme was the same—the story behind the murders—but the angles were different.

O. J. Simpson and the *National Enquirer*

O. J. Simpson first provoked *National Enquirer* readers in 1989 when Nicole Brown Simpson accused him of spousal abuse, "O. J. Beating Nicole; She Called Cops." Five years later when Nicole was murdered, the *Enquirer* resumed pressuring Simpson: "Cops: How O. J. Did It." "O. J.'s Knife: He Bought This Deadly Weapon just before Murders." "Inside in Her Handwriting . . . Nicole's Diary. O. J. Beat the Holy Hell out of Me and We Lied at the X-Ray Lab." Alan Butterfield, the reporter who obtained Nicole's diary, said, "The *National Enquirer* knows what to look for and what makes a story."

The *Enquirer* attacked the Simpson story like a team of experienced detectives investigating a murder case. From the *Enquirer* command center in Florida, Perel established a computer database that compiled and cross-checked information. The *Enquirer* was by far the leading news-gathering team among both mainstream and tabloid media covering the Simpson case. Frequently, the mainstream media looked to the *Enquirer* for accurate inside information. "From time to time, I gave them some exclusive material. They paid me back by going on TV or writing stories, admitting the *Enquirer* was getting all the best material," said Perel in "How *Enquirer* Scooped the World on O. J." David Margolick, a journalist for the *New York Times*, wrote in "The Enquirer: Required Reading in Simpson Case," "The *Enquirer* has probably shaped public perceptions of the case more than any other publication. In a story made for the tabloids, it stands head and shoulders above them all for aggressiveness and accuracy."

O. J. Simpson pleaded not guilty to both murders and was acquitted of all criminal charges, but the *Enquirer* continued its dogged pursuit of O. J. Simpson. The case was not over for the *Enquirer*; the story behind the murders remained untold. From the beginning, Perel said the *Enquirer* focused on the bloody shoe prints left by a man wearing size twelve Bruno Magli designer shoes, which were sold to fewer than three hundred customers in the United States. At the trial, Simpson denied owning "those ugly-ass shoes." After the trial, though, the *Enquirer* persisted in its investigation of the shoe clue, and successfully uncovered a photograph, later proven to be credible, of Simpson wearing Magli shoes. The photograph was entered as a key exhibit in the civil court proceedings that resulted in Simpson being held liable for the death of Ron Goldman.

O. J. Simpson and the *Star*

For those readers not interested in the *National Enquirer*'s detailed proceedings of the O. J. trial, the *Star* focused on the personal relationship theme, "O. J. & Nicole's Secret Wedding Video." The stories extended beyond O. J. Simpson and the murder victims to their friends, families, and all the players involved in their glamorous California lifestyle. "The O. J. story was the most incredible one I was ever

"Photo that Puts O. J. at Murder Scene"

Enclosed in a letter to the *National Enquirer* from a teenager in Colorado was an overexposed Polaroid photograph of the shadow of a person on a football field. Was it O. J. Simpson? Was he wearing Magli shoes? The photograph was inconclusive, but Larry Haley, the reporter on the story, said the teenager pointed out a logical conclusion that the *Enquirer* had missed—if Simpson owned the shoes he would have worn them to sporting events.

Over a period of six months the *Enquirer* staff worked backwards through hundreds of photographs sent in by photojournalists, comparing them with an enlarged photograph of the uniquely patterned sole of a Magli. One photograph, taken three years earlier at a professional football game in Buffalo, New York, showed Simpson walking with the distinctive sole of his shoe raised. Haley's job was to prove it was a Magli shoe.

To avoid partiality, only the shoe in the Simpson photograph was shown to a Magli shoe clerk, who confirmed that it was indeed a Magli. After comparing the shoe's sole in the photograph to the pattern visible in the court photographs of the footprint, a Metro Dade County Police Department expert concluded it was a match. At the Rochester Institute of Technology in Rochester, New York, a professor of photographic imagery confirmed that the photograph and the negatives were authentic. Thirty-three additional photographs further substantiated the claim that Simpson owned the Magli shoes.

The photograph and the *Enquirer* investigation survived the scrutiny of the mainstream media and the legal system. The teenager from Colorado received an unsolicited check from the *Enquirer*, its readers were presented with an exclusive, "Photo that Puts O. J. at Murder Scene," and Haley earned his second J. Edgar Hoover Award from the National Association of Police for "outstanding investigative reporting in the O. J. Simpson case."

O.J. IN THE MURDER

The ENQUIRER has uncovered blockbuster new proof that O.J. Simpson wore a pair of the rare shoes that left bloody footprints at his ex-wife's murder scene.

The disgraced gridiron great repeatedly denied ever owning the expensive Italian-made footwear.

But he flat-out lied!

In a photo tracked down by The ENQUIRER, Simpson is wearing the shoes just nine months before the brutal slayings of Nicole Simpson and her friend Ron Goldman.

FLASHBACK: The infamous bloody footprint as shown in court. The hand belongs to FBI agent William Bodziak.

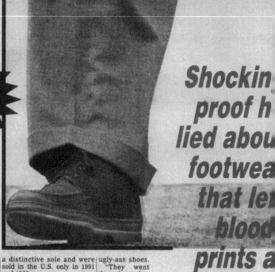

Shockin proof h lied abou footwea that le blood prints a death scen

During trial testimony, the FBI revealed less than 300 pairs of the shoe — a $160 lace-up style by designer Bruno Magli — were sold in Simpson's size 12 in the United States.

Prosecutors were unable to link Simpson to the murderer's shoes, which have a distinctive cross-hatched sole and are a size 12.

But in the photo, Simpson is taking a step forward, clearly showing the sole of one shoe — and it's an identical match to the bloody prints left at the murder scene.

"The photo that The ENQUIRER has uncovered is terrific evidence. It's a blockbuster!" declared famed New York attorney Raoul Felder, an expert on the Simpson murder case.

During Simpson's murder trial, FBI agent William Bodziak testified that the bloody shoe prints at the murder scene came from a pair of size 12 Bruno Magli shoes that had

a distinctive sole and were sold in the U.S. only in 1991 and 1992.

Simpson denied owning a pair of Bruno Magli shoes many times — including in his video and during a jailhouse meeting with his lawyers.

Simpson attorney Robert Shapiro wrote in his book "The Search for Justice" that when Simpson was shown similar shoes by his lawyers, he said: "I'd never wear those

ugly-ass shoes.

"They went through my closet. They know what kind of shoes I wear."

In his newly released video, the fallen football hero insisted: "First of all, I never would have worn those ugly shoes.

"The FBI did an exhaustive search about Bruno Magli shoes. They said it was a rare

shoe. They went to every let that sold Bruno M shoes. Not one person they ever sold me these B Magli shoes."

But he obviously own pair! The picture of Sim

MARTHA: The lifesty

Martha Stewart wants to give you a piece of her mind

Lifestyle guru Martha Stewart has a master plan to control your life — using her computer.

She plans to use the Internet to tell everyone from America to Zanzibar what to eat, what to wear, how to decorate their homes.

"She wants to control their minds with her ideas," said an insider.

"She sees herself as a super-guru who'll dominate how we live and what we do."

Martha already controls a $200-million media empire that includes a week-

tionally syndicated newspaper column and other ventures.

She revealed her Internet plans when she spoke to more than a thousand of her loyal followers — known as "Martha Wannabees" — in New York recently.

"It's called 'Ask Martha — the Household Helper,'" she said. "'Ask Martha' will be the household helper we ALL need.

"I'll have hundreds of researchers and computer programmers all over the world to answer any questions you may have.

"I want to inform, inspire and

a lifestyle is a good thing to do."

And Martha is the perfect person to tell all of us how to live because she's — well, perfect. Just ask her:

"I can't think of one thing I would change about myself," she told her followers.

"I see everything. I'm absolutely obsessively. I am in the driver's seat and it's a good place to be.

"If I got into a fight with Superman, I would win. I know his secret.

"Don't ever bet against me. I always win. I always get my way."

"O. J. in the Murder Shoes" *National Enquirer*™ April 23, 1996, pp. 8-9.

SHOES

© PHOTO/Gamma Liaison

SENSATIONAL PHOTO of O.J. in lace-up Bruno Magli shoes proves in close-up, above left, that he wore the expensive rare footwear he denied ever owning. The picture was taken Sept. 26, 1993, at the Bills-Dolphins football game in Buffalo. Below, photo of a Bruno Magli shoe shown in court during his murder trial.

Lorenzo

...aring the shoes was snap-
...d Sept. 26, 1993, at Rich
...dium in Buffalo, N.Y., dur-
...g a game between the Mia-
...Dolphins and the Buffalo
...lls.

...We took the sensational pho-
...to a Bruno Magli shoe store
...Boca Raton, Fla., and
...owed it to manager Stephen
...ith.

..."That's our Lorenzo 1 mod-
..." he said.

...The sole was made of "a
...bber-like composite called
...ga," Smith added.

..."The silga sole, a distinct
...oss-hatched pattern, is a
...an-made composite.

..."The shoe in your photo of
...J. Simpson is definitely our
...renzo 1 model. The match
...the sole is perfect."

...We also showed the photo to
...bert Hart, an expert wit-
...ss often called by Metro
...de Police in Miami, Fla., for
...otographic identification of
...twear in court.

...Hart compared the pic-
...e with a photo chart of
...uno Magli's Lorenzo 1
...oe that prosecutors
...owed the jury. The chart
...oved that the shoe's sole
...atched the bloody prints

left at the murder scene.

"The shoe appears identical to the Bruno Magli Lorenzo on the chart," said Hart, owner of Florida Forensic Photography in Miami.

Smith added: "The Lorenzo 1 model is a very rare and unusual shoe. No other shoes in the world have that distinct cross-hatched pattern."

The stork almost land-
ed on the rooftop
of Tony Randall's
dreams, but at the last moment the flight was delayed.

A few weeks ago, the "Odd Couple's" Felix Unger and his lovely new wife Heather were overjoyed, convinced she was expecting his first-ever child.

"We thought she was preg-nant for a little while and we were both hoping and looking at the calendar, but it didn't turn out," disappointed Tony, 76, told The ENQUIRER.

"Now, we'll wait and see what happens next month."

Tony and Heather, 25, mar-ried last November 17. His first wife Florence died in 1992

HEATHER and TONY
Still trying

after 53 years of marriage, and they had no children.

"Children are the only thing in life I have missed out on," Tony told The ENQUIRER. "My wife wants children too, so I would love to have them.

"I've read in the newspa-pers that we are going to fer-tility doctors and all of that. None of that stuff is true. We're not doing anything spe-cial — just loving each other. Whatever happens, happens."

Tony is in New York under-studying two roles and acting as producer in the Tony Ran-dall National Actors Theater production of "Inherit the Wind," starring Charles Durn-ing and George C. Scott.

"I've been really busy, but we're definitely going to keep trying," he said. "I want to be a father and I am planning on it. I'd like to have a little girl who looks just like my wife.

"But if we have a little boy, that would be just fine with me too!"
— **JOHN BLOSSER**

9

NATIONAL ENQUIRER

"O. J. Didn't Do It" *Globe*™ July 19, 1994.

involved in," said Steven LeGrice, who covered the story. "It was like an onion, it peeled off in layers."

The *Star* asked, how were the Simpson children coping, what did Nicole's sisters and girlfriends think of O. J., and what kind of parties did their group attend? If Simpson was guilty, what drove him to do it, what did Nicole do to push his button? But when the *Star* wrote a story about "Nicole's Tragic Addiction to Sex," their women readers protested. You have gone too far, they said, Nicole's murder was not her fault.

O. J. Simpson and the *Globe*

The *Globe* pursued a position contrary to that of the *Enquirer*; "O. J. Didn't Do It!" Either way, guilty or innocent, O. J. was "money in the bank," said Phil Bunton, its editor-in-chief. Typically, the *Globe* offered reward money as an added incentive: "Who Framed O. J.? $1 Million Reward." Although Simpson's legal defense team did not require help from the *Globe*'s readers, everyone who wanted a chance to collect the reward bought the *Globe*.

Three-quarters of the way through the trial, Bunton left the *Globe* to take over as executive editor of the *Star*. His previous contacts with the O. J. Simpson team followed him and offered Simpson's exclusive story for one million dollars if he was acquitted. Within twenty-four hours of his acquittal, Simpson gave the *Star* an interview. Two weeks later it published, "O. J.'s Joyful Homecoming . . . Dozens of Fabulous Intimate Photos," the first of a proposed four-part series—a series that stopped at two. The reaction from a public angry and divided over the verdict was so fierce that the *Star* hired security guards to protect its newsroom, and grocery store owners hid the issues in storage areas.

In 1995 the O. J. Simpson trial concluded, midway through what had been referred to by David Kamp as the "Tabloid Decade," a decade of "prevailing national interest in sex, death, celebrity and televised car chases." Celebrity gossip was everywhere and was instantaneously accessible—it saturated television, the Internet, and mainstream print media. Tabloid Valley faced a major challenge from an expanded field of mainstream media competitors that had gone tabloid.

"O. J.'s Joyful Homecoming" *Star*™ October 17, 1995.

Chapter 7

The Influence of Tabloid Valley

"IF ELVIS WAS DEAD he'd be rolling in his grave," said Steven LeGrice, former executive editor of the *Star*. During the tabloid decade of the 1990s the celebrity tabloids were not abandoning Hollywood, but the hint of a political scandal emanating from Washington, D.C., reminded them of the national recognition and huge circulation sales that the *National Enquirer* earned with its momentous 1987 exposé of Senator Gary Hart's extramarital entanglement. "As tabloids we pursued scandal in whatever form it took . . . any sort of scandal would sell magazines. It could be an evangelical sex scandal; it could be sexual hijinks in the Supreme Court," said Phil Bunton, veteran tabloid editor.

A Washington Scandal

One of the recurring themes explored in tabloid stories is the abrupt rise and fall, and sometimes redemption, of the famous and powerful. In 1996, four years after the *Star* published the diaries and tapes documenting Gennifer Flowers's alleged affair with 1992 Democratic presidential candidate Bill Clinton, it returned to Clinton's circle to expose allegations of a sex scandal involving President Clinton's valued political strategist and consultant, Dick Morris. Morris, referred to by *Time* magazine as "The Man Who Has Clinton's Ear," strongly influenced the family-values agenda for the Clinton presidency. A low-profile man behind the president, Morris hardly seemed the type to turn up in "Hooker's Sizzling Love Diaries," until the *Star's* exposé made him a tabloid celebrity. The *Star* anticipated what its readers wanted.

This time, instead of having to trace down five elusive women named in a lawsuit, the *Star* had only to sit back and listen to a woman with a story to tell. Sherry Rowlands, a $200-an-hour prostitute, claimed she and Morris shared a long-term secret relationship. Initially, the *Star* was not particularly interested in the alleged sexual indiscretion of yet another politician. Admittedly, prostitution was illegal and Morris was a married family man, but there the scandal appeared to end—at least until Rowlands produced diaries and taped telephone conversations that carried ramifications of a greater than sexual nature. Then the *Star* became interested. Did Morris share information of national security with a prostitute? What secrets did he divulge? What classified items did she learn of when Morris allowed her to eavesdrop on his private conversations with the president? She had a marketable commodity to sell the tabloid.

"There was a good circumstantial case, but nothing that absolutely nailed it," said Richard Goodling, the reporter on the story, in an interview with *Time*. It needed "visual confirmation," proof that required patience, stratagems, and long-range photographic equipment that the *Star* quickly secured. Holed up in a hotel room, *Star* staff waited ten days for the arranged rendezvous. As Rowlands and Morris, garbed in matching hotel bathrobes, embraced on their balcony, photographers recorded the scene from another balcony. Did this constitute entrapment? No, the *Star* contended; it was not creating a relationship, it was merely confirming one.

On Friday, August 30, before the conclusion of the 1996 Democratic Presidential Convention in Chicago, the *New York Post* publicized the impending story, crediting the *Star*. The weekly *Star* gave a small teaser of its full story, "White House Call Girl Scandal," to the daily *Post* to protect their exclusive. Since the *Star's* story was printed on Tuesday but would not appear on the supermarket racks until the following Sunday or Monday, they were placed in a vulnerable position. At least two mainstream newspapers were aware of the scandal brewing, but skeptical of the source, they chose not to print it. Not so, the *Post*—it bestowed upon the teaser the full tabloid treatment of a Page One story, delivering the hype without giving away the exclusive details, which were reserved for the *Star*. "We knew they (the *New York Post*) were the most likely to give the story a good play the next morning," said former executive editor Phil Bunton. "We wanted the maximum bang for our buck."

Morris's only response was to accuse the *Star* in the *New York Times* of "the sadistic vitriol of yellow journalism." He gave no interviews, and resigned the night before President Clinton's acceptance speech. "As happened so often during the O. J. Simpson trial, the mainstream press had to acknowledge that the tabloids, and tabloid tactics, can sometimes unearth legitimate news. And the *Star* got another notch in its gun belt," wrote Richard Zoglin in *Time* magazine.

A True Crime Story that Will Not Disappear

The supermarket tabloids feel vindicated when they receive positive acknowledgment for a credible story from the mainstream media, but more important are the boosted sales generated by breaking a big story. In 1996, the big story was the murder of 6-year-old beauty pageant contestant JonBenet Ramsey. Mainstream media sources competed with the tabloids by covering the many speculations about and extraneous facets of the sensational homicide case. In lieu of actually investigating the crime, the media named suspects, scrutinized the victim's family, exhibited pageant photographs of the victim, vividly described the crime scene, and worked contacts for juicy inside information.

The first week after the murder, the *Globe* published confidential autopsy and crime scene photographs, obtained by an inside source. In Boulder, Colorado, local news outlets boycotted the *Globe*, but citizens simply drove outside the city limits to buy a copy of the must-read issue. A few weeks later, the *Globe*, its reputation tarnished by its crass display of the autopsy photos, offered a five hundred thousand dollar reward for information leading to the conviction of the murderer. The reward money was never claimed, but the publicity attracted curious readers who ignored the competition's skepticism about the *Globe*'s motives.

When the crime remained unsolved, speculation prevented this story "with legs" from losing momentum. Three years after the murder, the *National Enquirer* tallied, "Beauty Queen Murder, Week #126." Ten years after the commission of the crime, a suspect was arrested, and in the race to get out a spectacular story, national and international, mainstream and tabloid media rushed to solve the case, mainly by making loose assumptions. Within a week, the suspect was released after DNA samples did not match those taken at the scene of the crime. The *Enquirer* was prepared with a nine-page inside spread, "JonBenet Murder Suspect, He Didn't Do It." The following week the *National Examiner* rewrote the story, "The Real JonBenet Killer!—& It's Not Wacko who Confessed!" By 2007, the killer still had not been caught and the big story remained untold.

The Tabloids and Reward Money

The *Globe*'s reward did not aid in capturing the perpetrator and the story of the JonBenet Ramsey murder, but in 1997 the *National Enquirer* was quite successful when it offered a reward of $100,000 for information leading to the conviction of the murderer of actor Bill Cosby's son, Ennis Cosby. Among the thousands of would-be informants who flooded the *Enquirer*'s hotline, one witness claimed to know the

A Back Story

A back story is the story behind the news story, the story that does not get printed but is often interesting in and of itself. It consists of extraneous, unsubstantiated, or inappropriate material. At the time of the Ramsey murder investigation, a back story circulated in the tabloid rumor mill regarding the purported exploits of two overseas tabloid reporters. Motivated by intense competition, the journalists concocted a scheme to bug the house of the victim's family. They would send the Ramseys an oversized bouquet of condolence flowers containing a wireless microphone, which would communicate with a transmitter located in an ice cream vendor truck the two would lease and pretend to operate.

Between dipping extra-large servings of ice cream, the reporters listened to a static-filled conversation transmitted by the microphone. They had hoped for inside information about the murder investigation; instead, they learned what the Ramseys' neighbors ate for breakfast. Since the grieving mother was allergic to flowers, she had sent the bouquet next door.

Irrefutably, this is illegal, "over-the-top" news-gathering, but the tale of the back story epitomizes the tabloid frenzy occurring behind the scenes of an internationally followed murder investigation. What would a publication do with information obtained illegally? If it heard, "I won't rest until I find her killer," a particularly daring tabloid might find a way to publish it, "as told by a friend or housekeeper." If it overheard a confession by the murderer—"I killed her"—it could not use it. And so this back story went into the scrap pile and tabloid rumor mill.

location of the murder weapon and the name of the murderer. The informant, Christopher So, led the Los Angeles Police investigators to a field where they found a gun—verified to be the murder weapon—that was eventually traced to the suspect. Even in jail, the suspect did not gain immunity from the *Enquirer*'s probe. A reporter flushed out a source that produced incriminating letters written by the accused, "Cosby Killer's Written Confession from Jail."

Mr. So returned home to wait for his reward. In Lantana, Steven Coz, the editor-in-chief, and David Perel, the lead editor, atypically sat on their exclusive until the trial was concluded and they could publish their interview with Mr. So, the key witness. The murder trial was low-key, deliberately void of excessive media coverage, and the suspect was found guilty. In contrast, the *Enquirer*'s reward ceremony was a public relations production attended by national media. Wearing a sports cap inscribed with "Enquiring Minds," Mr. So accepted his poster-sized check.

"What was most notable about the trial was that it might not have taken place at all were it not for the efforts (and deep pockets) of the nation's most widely read supermarket tabloid," wrote Jodie Morse in *Time* magazine. But journalist Christian Berthelsen in the *New York Times* said, "The *Enquirer*'s reward posed troubling questions: Does it undermine the credibility of the government witness by allowing the defense to argue, as it has, that he was motivated by financial gain? And does it encourage crime witnesses to hold out for the biggest payday before cooperating with authorities?" Payment notwithstanding, the information was well-founded and the *Enquirer* helped catch a killer. Berthelson continued, "While recognizing the potential inducement for embellishment, Mr. Coz said that the police investigation backed up Mr. So's tip and that he did not think the reward offer would have a longer-lasting negative impact on the justice system."

The Influence of the *National Enquirer*

"The *National Enquirer* is on a roll," announced *Time* magazine upon their selection of *Enquirer* editor-in-chief Steve Coz as one of "*Time's* 25 Most Influential Americans" in 1997. Why would a tabloid, once thought of as scurrilous and gory, receive national accolades for a job well done? "Going back before the O. J. Simpson case to the incriminating photos of Gary Hart and Donna Rice, the *National Enquirer* required mainstream media to react and respond," said Roy Peter Clark of the Poytner Institute for Journalism. *Time* cited the detailed coverage of the O. J. Simpson investigation and criminal trial, as well as the photograph of the Bruno Magli shoes submitted as key evidence in the Simpson civil jury trial as examples of influential stories of the 1990s initially disclosed by the *Enquirer* and pursued by the mainstream media. David Perel, current editor-in-chief of the *Enquirer*, said, "What made the difference in the O. J. Simpson coverage by the *National Enquirer* from the mainstream was singular focus and old fashioned reporting—knocking on doors, going on foot to chase down every potential lead. That's the DNA of the *National Enquirer*, the hallmark of the *National Enquirer's* heritage."

"Coz, 39, is one of a new breed of editors who are making the tabs more influential," elaborated the editors of *Time*. Although celebrity gossip continued to figure prominently in supermarket tabloids' content, Coz and his breed represented a shift in editorial priorities, "aggressively pursuing the stories that end up on the evening news."

Were the *National Enquirer* and its companion celebrity tabloids becoming as respectable as mainstream media outlets? After all, tabloid reporters pursue their quarry with a vengeance and skill that often produce a credible national news story. But the glow of these accolades is a bit dimmed in the eyes of many because they distrust the bearer of the tale, the supermarket tabloids that pay for information.

On the other hand, was the mainstream media exhibiting more tabloid sensationalism? "Every single network, every single magazine in America has gone more celebrity," said Coz in a *Time* interview. "That's the *Enquirer's* influence, whether you like it or don't like it . . . Our role is to get to the truth of what these people who become icons are really like."

"Rock Solid Tabloid" in Boca Raton

While the *National Enquirer* strove to broaden its range of readers with a new degree of respectability, Boca Raton's *Globe* was a "rock-solid tabloid," said former editor Tony Frost in an interview with *US* magazine. Ultimately the *Globe* and the *Enquirer* clashed over a typical tabloid story telling of a happily married husband and family man who was reportedly led astray by another woman. The *Globe* claimed it was exposing a scandal; the *Enquirer* accused it of creating a scandal with sexual entrapment.

The story involved an alleged flirtation between a sportscaster, Frank Gifford, and a former flight attendant, Suzen Johnson. The *Globe* had already taken down Johnson's story, but it still needed an incriminating photograph. Johnson was only paid for her exclusive interview, not to seduce Gifford, the *Globe* insisted. Nevertheless, videotaped and recorded, "10 Sizzling Photos Expose His Sex Romps with Blonde in Hotel Love Nest" incited Steve Coz to distance the *Enquirer* from the *Globe*. Coz took his cause straight to the top of the mainstream news in an article he wrote for the *New York Times* titled, "When Tabloids Cross the Line," in which he says, "Chasing news is fine but staging it is not."

A year later, Johnson approached the *Enquirer* with a revised version of her story that claimed she had been paid two hundred and fifty thousand dollars to help entrap the sportscaster. The *Globe* sued her for breach of an exclusive contract, whereupon she countersued the *Globe* and hired her own publicist. In yet another legal maneuvering, the *Globe* sued the *Enquirer* in an effort to halt publication of her story. The legal staffs of the two tabloids met in court to settle their differences. Each left the courthouse with a story for their readers; the *Enquirer* published Johnson's retold story, and the *Globe*, their rebuttal.

A Tabloid Backlash

While the supermarket tabloids jostled for ascendancy over Tabloid Valley, an international tragedy triggered a tabloid backlash that reverberated across the Atlantic Ocean from Europe to North America. On August 31, 1997, Diana the Princess of Wales and her companion Dodi Fayed died in a car accident in Paris, France. First on the scene were celebrity-chasing European photographers, the paparazzi, who had been in close pursuit of the car carrying the famous couple, trying to obtain a photograph to sell to the media. Only two weeks earlier, an Italian photographer had earned one million dollars for "The Kiss," a photograph of Princess Diana and Dodi Fayed kissing on the deck of Fayed's yacht.

The paparazzi, greedy to the last, leaned into the mangled vehicle and snapped photographs of the dying victims. "Death photos," *USA Today* called them. "Blood money," said Phil Bunton, executive editor at the *Star*. "We will not bid on them," said David Perel, at the time executive editor of the *National Enquirer*. "We're urging the world media to join us in not buying them." Not all of the world's media corporations resisted a sensational photo, but in an unusual instance of unofficial solidarity, American mainstream media and the tabloids agreed to reject any photographs showing the bodies trapped in the car.

Yet in spite of their restraint, the supermarket tabloids incurred some immediate damage. The night of the fatal accident, the weekly preassembled issue of the *Enquirer* appeared in stores, "Di Goes Sex Mad, I Can't Get Enough!" The *Enquirer* apologized and the issues were pulled from distribution. The *Globe*, too, was caught by its weekly deadline. On an inside page of its latest issue an unfortunate choice of words emphasized a photograph of a glamorous Diana in a swimsuit, "To Di For!"

Across the board, throughout Princess Diana's lifetime, the tabloids chronicled the intimate details of her life, "*Star* Exclusive: Di's Shocking Bedroom Secrets (Banned in Britain), Blockbuster New Book by Royal Housekeeper." Upon Diana's death, the supermarket tabloids heeded the wishes of their readers and offered pages of tributes, without a hint of a scandal.

The backlash was a surprise. Usually the death of a celebrity is as important a tabloid theme as a wedding. In 1982, when Princess Grace of Monaco died in an automobile accident, the *National Enquirer* sent thirty reporters to the scene. "Grace: The Real Story, She Didn't Have to Die—the Only Picture of the Crash—Her Last Words—to the Only Person who Saw the Accident" sold over six million copies for the *Enquirer*, second only in sales to the issue featuring Elvis Presley in his coffin. A team comprised of one *Star* staff reporter, Peter Williams, and a few freelancers was outnumbered, as usual, by that sent in by the *Enquirer*, but nevertheless, the *Star* produced an exclusive, "Princess Grace, 2 Dramatic Exclusives: Stephanie's Own Story of Crash. Did I Cause Grace's Death—Truck Driver's Anguish." Sales reached almost five million, making the issue a tremendous success for the *Star*. Rupert Murdoch thanked his staff by sending them on a trip to Puerto Rico.

More than a decade later when Princess Diana died, the circumstances of her death raised the question of whether the car accident may have been caused by overly-aggressive paparazzi instigating a high-speed car chase. Who was responsible? The paparazzi who supplied the demand for celebrity photographs? The media who paid a premium for such photos and whetted the public's appetite for celebrity news? Or the celebrity-worshipping public themselves, who demanded to know a celebrity's most intimate secrets? Steve Coz, as editor-in-chief of the *National Enquirer*, said in an interview with *Time* magazine, "We told (a year ago) the paparazzi we didn't want

PRINCESS

Star GRACE

OCTOBER 5, 1982
45¢

2 DRAMATIC EXCLUSIVES

●Stephanie's own story of crash

●Did I cause Grace's death? —truck driver's anguish

CAROLINE GRIEVES FOR HER MOTHER

STAR SPECIAL 10-PAGE TRIBUTE

FUNERAL: MOVING COLOR PHOTO REPORT

PLUS
●The last color family portraits
●The last interview

BOOK EXTRA
THREE GREAT LOVES OF GRACE

"Princess Grace" *Star*™ October 5, 1982.

"Grace, the Real Story" *National Enquirer*™ October 5, 1982.

stalking pictures." Nevertheless, the repugnance the American public felt about the paparazzi's methods was directed against the supermarket tabloids, and the impact was a decline in circulation sales and public perception.

A Taste of Their Own Medicine

The supermarket tabloids' sentimental coverage of Princess Diana following her death pleased loyal readers, but Hollywood's celebrities were not so easily placated. Actors George Clooney and Tom Cruise led a crusade against supermarket tabloids, asking the public to boycott them. The public did not.

Reportedly, a group of actors hired a private detective to investigate three tabloid editors—Steve Coz at the National Enquirer, Tony Frost at the Globe, and Phil Bunton at the Star—to see how they liked being watched. "Whether I'm paranoid or not, I did see someone parked (lights off) just down the street from my home for a few days around that time," said Phil Bunton. "But nothing ever happened."

The Supermarket Tabloids Rebound

There is no doubt that the year following Princess Diana's death was a difficult one for supermarket tabloids, especially those for which celebrity stories were the main selling point. The *National Enquirer* turned to its special project team to revive sales. Several years earlier in 1990, the *Enquirer* had sold nearly one million copies of a 76-page magazine, "Stars' Diet Secrets," a collection of celebrities' favorite diets. Mike Nevard was recruited as the editor for the Special Projects Department. He and his staff worked from a trailer in the backyard of the *Enquirer* office complex to produce a series of individual specials, composed for release every five weeks. "Soap Opera Secrets" sold over

Hurricane Planning Center

The *National Enquirer*'s Special Projects trailer was in its own little world, hidden from the main newsroom by a grove of tropical trees. A chimney jutted from the top of the trailer to vent the cigar smoke which filled Mike Nevard's editorial office. The trailer doubled as the clearinghouse for the UK edition and the headquarters for the *National Enquirer*'s Hurricane Planning Center, created after Hurricane Andrew, a category four storm, struck South Florida in 1992. With the communication and transportation infrastructure in tatters following the hurricane, the *Enquirer* scrambled to continue production. Desperate, its editors traveled to the *Star*'s offices in Tarrytown, New York, to complete the upcoming issue. Subsequently, it was Nevard's job to oversee comprehensive hurricane plans were made to ensure minimal interruption in output. "I think that small piece of property is worth its weight in gold," said Nevard in the company publication, "The Insider, News for the Employees of *Enquirer/Star* Group."

nine hundred thousand copies. "Scandals of the Rich and Famous" broke the one million mark. In total, successive issues of these specials netted over eleven million sales. Thereafter, Nevard was known as the "11,000,000-copy man."

Globe Communications responded with Mini Mags, started by Michael Rosenbloom as a profitable sideline in the 1980s and expanded by former editor Billy Burt to become an integral part of AMI's side publications. 3" wide and 4" high, the subjects explored in Mini Mags ranged from weight loss advice and arthritis cures to astrological predictions and ghost stories. Occasionally a weightier subject required a larger Mini Mag, about half the size of a piece of paper and approximately thirty-six thousand words. "No Bad Dogs," a large Mini

Mag written by Emily Hamer-West, was so successful that a Canadian animal shelter in Vancouver ordered fifteen hundred copies to hand out with adopted dogs. "Essentially the book was about how there's no such thing as a bad dog, just untrained dogs," she said.

Bat Boy, Ed Anger, and Elvis Was Alive

AMI's wildly imaginative *Weekly World News* seemed to be immune to the Princess Diana backlash. It celebrated the discovery of "Bat Child Found in Cave! His Giant Eyes See in the Dark & His Ears Are Better Than Radar, Say Scientists." Half bat, half boy, this adventurous and quirky character, drawn by graphics artist Dick Kulpa, roamed the globe, riding the New York subway, falling in love, and fighting terrorists.

Rafe Klinger, a former Chicago schoolteacher, created "I'm pig-biting mad" Ed Anger, the "most irresponsibly berserk columnist in America," according to *Rolling Stone*. Was violence out of control in our public schools? Anger replied with his typical black humor, "Make Every Kid Pack a Pistol!"

Spectacularly, Elvis was alive, first sighted in Michigan in 1984, later in Texas, and then Canada. He periodically reappeared to keep the story going and boost circulation sales. "Elvis Is Alive . . . That Was a Double in My Coffin!" was the first issue of the *Weekly World News* to sell a million copies.

Former editor Joe West recalled that his managing editor Eddie Clontz had received an anonymous letter from a reader saying she had seen Elvis at a Burger King in Michigan, having a triple cheeseburger and a strawberry shake.

Eddie said to me: "Hey, let's do an Elvis is alive story."
I answered: "Hell, no. Who's going to believe that crap?"
"Maybe a million people."

FIRST PHOTO OF 2-FOOT-TALL CREATURE!

Boy captured by explorers 2 miles underground!

WEEKLY WORLD NEWS

85¢/95¢ CANADA

June 23, 1992

BAT CHILD FOUND IN CAVE!

HIS GIANT EYES SEE IN THE DARK & HIS EARS ARE BETTER THAN RADAR, SAY SCIENTISTS

"Bat Child Found In Cave" *Weekly World News*™ June 23, 1992.

"Nah," I said, "it's crapola. Elvis is as dead as a doorknob."

Eddie scribbled the "Elvis Is Alive!" headline on a scrap of paper and handed it to me. "Trust me, that should be our page one for next week."

My reply was to crumple up the paper and throw it in the garbage can.

An hour later, Elvis preying on my fevered brain, I dug the paper out of the garbage. "You're right, Eddie," I said. "That's our headline for next week."

. . . and the rest, as they say, is history.

Nellie Mitchell

Tabloid readers angry at the celebrity tabloids accepted the *Weekly World News* and the *Sun* as mischievous but harmless entertainment. The nugget of truth embedded in the stories was so scrambled with fabrications that these tabloids thought no one could or would accuse them of libel. For instance, former staff writer Joe West inserted a family photo of his beautiful baby daughter between the arms of a gorilla for "Ape Gives Birth to Human Baby." But Nellie Mitchell, a 97-year-old woman from St. Louis, Missouri, took the *Sun* to court for "Oldest Newspaper Carrier, 101, Quits Because She's Pregnant!" The photograph of the pregnant newspaper carrier was that of Nellie, albeit doctored heavily. Thinking Nellie was deceased, the *Sun* lifted an old photograph of her from a newspaper file and set the story in Australia. Unfortunately for the *Sun*, but fortunately for Nellie, the elderly woman was very much alive and was sharp enough to retain a lawyer and collect eight hundred and fifty thousand dollars in punitive damages.

"Ape Gives Birth To Human Baby" *Sun*™ March 17, 1992.

TOH Stories

While the big three—the *Star*, the *National Enquirer*, and the *Globe*—
and the mainstream press, also not exempt from capitalizing on celebrity photographs, analyzed their role in harmful paparazzi tactics, the
National Examiner, lacking the resources to be a serious contender
for breaking news, concentrated on filling in story gaps for its weekly
issue. "In desperation we HAD to come up with ideas for stories," said
Al Fayette, former assistant editor.

TOH is tabloidese for "Top of Head." "In other words these stories are just pulled from the top of your head," said former tabloid
reporter John Harris. Using Hurricane Andrew (a deadly storm that
made landfall in South Florida in 1992) as a backdrop for the absur-
dity of a TOH story, Fayette wove a tale about a dog blown from Miami to Louisiana. "The dog landed in some small parish in Louisiana
where it was taken to a veterinarian, pronounced 'safe and sound'
and returned to its owner in Miami," said Fayette in an interview. The
day after the story was published in the *Examiner*, the *Miami Herald* called to interview the dog's owner. "But I told the *Miami Herald*
reporter that the vet didn't want his name used," Fayette said. "And,
I'd see if the owners were available for interviews. I never got back to
him."

In 1993 a newly installed editor at the *Examiner* instructed his writers to eliminate TOH stories. In Tabloid Valley it was not unusual for
an editor to change jobs several times, either within a given organization or to a competing one. As part of the changeover, different editors typically adjusted the operation to accommodate their personal
philosophy and the latest circulation figures. An interoffice memo
described the editor's vision of "the New *Examiner*." No more, "Elvis
Ghost Sings in My Vacuum Cleaner." Instead, the *Examiner* tried an
updated approach to attract women readers, "Oh Baby! How to Be a
'90s Mom."

The White House Scandal

The supermarket celebrity tabloids bore the brunt of the Princess Diana backlash in America, but the greatest threat to their status as purveyors of celebrity gossip occurred when mainstream news organizations and other tabloids began covering the same stories. In 1998 "The Siren" at the top of the webpage www.DrudgeSiren.com, companion site of the Internet's *Drudge Report*, signaled the breaking news of an alleged sex scandal involving a White House intern, Monica Lewinsky, and President Bill Clinton. *Newsweek* was actually the first to receive the information, but it deliberated for a week about whether to broach the sensitive subject, too long for the allegations to remain a secret.

The *National Enquirer*, the *Star*, and the *Globe* competed with a huge media contingent that converged on Little Rock, Arkansas, and Washington, D.C. Mainstream Washington correspondents tapped into their extensive network of home contacts. Rumors, allegations, and details of explicit sexual acts exposed during the televised investigation propagated through online gossip sites, broadcast news, and mainstream news publications. "The story that caromed off the keyboard of an Internet tipster and hurtled through the talk shows to the top of every network news broadcast and major newspaper in the country appears to many in journalism to have blurred the boundaries between mainstream and tabloid news," wrote Janny Scott in the *New York Times*.

The challenge for the supermarket tabloids was to create a fresh angle every week before information from another media source overshadowed their story. As with the O. J. Simpson investigation, the *National Enquirer*, the *Star*, and the *Globe* experimented with reporting different takes on the scandal. On February 10, 1998, the *Star* revealed Monica's story, "Monica's Own Story. Affair Started on Day We Met—after I Flashed My Sexy Underwear." The *Globe* wrote, "How Lovestruck Monica Stalked the President . . . Fatal Attraction!" The

"Clinton The Cheating, Lying, Dirty Phone Calls & Steamy Sex" *National Enquirer*™ February 10, 1998.

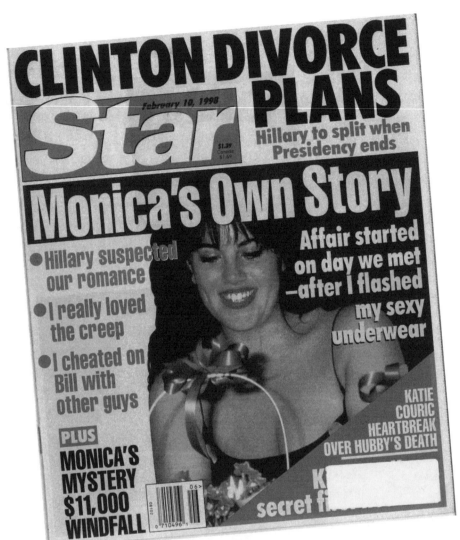

"Monica's Own Story" *Star*™ February 10, 1998.

Enquirer blamed the president, "Clinton the Cheating, Lying, Dirty Phone Calls & Steamy Sex."

Exclusives were elusive. The *Star* offered Lewinsky one million dollars for her exclusive story, but was outdone in what became a bidding war between commercial book publishers. In an interview with the *Palm Beach Post*, *Enquirer* editor-in-chief Steve Coz "lamented that most of the details have already been leaked, leaving little news for readers." Filmmaker and writer John Waters said in *Vanity Fair*, "My sense is that they (the tabloids) hate the Monica story because they've been robbed of it. They feel gypped. It should be theirs and it's everyone's."

AMI Consolidates

Competition in the swollen media marketplace reversed the growth of Florida's supermarket tabloids, and the flagship *National Enquirer*, most successful of them all, accordingly experienced the most dramatic decline. In 1977 the *Enquirer* sold more than six million copies of the issue featuring a photograph of a dead Elvis Presley in his coffin. By 1989, however, the average sales of the *Enquirer* had dropped to a little over four million issues a week, from whence they slid further to less than three million by 1995. Four years later in 1999, average circulation sales of the *Enquirer* hovered at slightly over two million.

But Generoso Pope Jr.'s distribution system, DSI, enticed investors. DSI was, and remains, a major magazine distributing arm of AMI that controls 65 percent of all "pockets," the racks at supermarket checkout counters where magazines and tabloids are displayed for sale. In February of 1999, MacFadden Holdings Inc. and the Boston venture capital group sold AMI for $767 million to Thomas H. Lee Partners Inc. and Evercore Capital Partners. The following November, the new owners of AMI consolidated their position as sole proprietors of Tabloid Valley by purchasing Globe Communications for $105 million. Six supermarket tabloids—the *National Enquirer*, the *Star*, the *Globe*,

National Enquirer building as a charter school, Attachment 3. (Courtesy of Tom Wilbur.)

the *National Examiner*, the *Weekly World News*, and the *Sun*—now operated under the direction of one corporate entity, AMI, headquartered in the former Globe Communications building in Boca Raton and led by Chairman and Chief Executive Officer David J. Pecker. AMI took the traditional corporate formula of maximizing profits by cutting operational costs a step further when it moved the *National Enquirer*, Lantana's most famous resident, to Boca Raton, where it was joined by the *Star* from Tarrytown, New York. By the beginning of the new millennium, the consolidation of Tabloid Valley had been completed.

Chapter 8

Tabloid Valley Enters the New Millennium

"IT'S GOING TO BE open warfare. How we're all going to work to-gether, I don't know. It's like putting the Bosnians, Croats, Jews and Arabs all together in the same area. We've spent the last thirty years or more hating each other's guts, and now we're going to be sharing the same cafeteria and day-care center," said Phil Bunton, *Star* execu-tive editor in a newspaper interview in 1999. The *Star*, announced the new owners of AMI, would no longer chase celebrity gossip from its newsroom in Tarrytown, New York. Instead, it would join its tabloid colleagues in Boca Raton, Florida. "I think it will be a big plus," said CEO David Pecker to the *Palm Beach Post*. "I'm trying to build one competitive spirit."

A logical assumption is that the cutthroat competition that spurred the *Enquirer*, the *Star*, and the *Globe* to produce the groundbreaking scoops that made tabloids famous would create synergy when housed beneath one roof and directed towards a common goal. The fault in this assumption is that a collaborative effort in place of a competitive one might instead stifle motivation and resourcefulness. A premoni-tion of these challenges occurred in the spring of 2000, when fewer than ten of the sixty *Star* employees elected to move with their jobs to Florida and participate in the Tabloid Valley corporate makeover.

Consolidating the six major Tabloid Valley weeklies at a central location in Boca Raton was one aspect of AMI's master plan. In July of 1999, soon after Thomas H. Lee Partners Inc. and Evercore Capital Partners purchased AMI and Globe Communications, CEO David Pecker, formerly a publishing executive at Hachette Filippachi Media U.S.A., spoke at the Palm Beach Chamber of Commerce. "I want to build the largest consumer publishing company in the United States, and I want to build it right here in Palm Beach County." In February 2000, Pecker outlined for the media a growth strategy that included an "acquisition binge" of additional consumer magazine publications and a revitalization of the core supermarket tabloids. Through the purchase of Weider Publications, AMI acquired seven health and fitness magazines. In 2003 its publications totaled six tabloids, twelve magazines, and two hundred mini booklets and digests.

With more and more acquisitions, AMI's revenue and debt increased. Reducing operating costs by consolidating the editorial division into one facility and increasing cash flow by raising the newsstand prices of its publications improved AMI's financial outlook, but Pecker anticipated increased income from the creation of www.gossip.com, a celebrity news website, and from broadcasting televised editions of the *Weekly World News* and the *National Enquirer*, which would be produced and promoted by an in-house television production studio and advertising agency. These proposed ventures would have proven quite costly, and for unpublicized reasons, AMI elected to forgo the hybrid tabloid-television field and limit their Internet presence to individual websites for the *Star*, the *Enquirer*, and the *Weekly World News*. These websites offered teasers of each publication's weekly stories to entice web browsers into buying the tabloid.

Whereas buying additional publications is time-consuming and ties up money, creating new publications from an in-place publishing operation is cost-effective and efficient. Pecker tapped into an experienced editorial staff, an established printing division, and a powerful distribution system to create a leadoff batch of three new magazines. *Mira!*, a Spanish version of the *National Enquirer*, *Auto World Weekly*, and *Country Weekly* were each intended to address a different niche market, but they met with little success, and *Auto World Weekly* was rather quickly discontinued. By 2007 the remaining two magazines were offered for sale, but an uninterested publishing market turned up no buyers, so they remained part of AMI. The biggest surprise was *Mira!*'s relatively bland reception, for expectations that Hispanic women who grew up with the spicy tabloids of Latin America would flock to it had run high. Perhaps the *Enquirer*, toned down for American supermarkets, was not hot enough.

Supported by the AMI distribution outlet, DSI, the six supermarket tabloids retained their prominent positions at the supermarket sales racks, but they no longer represented the sole source of tabloid entertainment. There were Internet gossip sites and blogs, celebrity magazines, the mainstream press, and tabloid television to feed the public's appetite for personality-driven news. "The focus has changed to more gossipy," said David Perel, current editor-in-chief of the *National Enquirer*. Theoretically, numerous outlets pushing celebrity news generates heightened interest, which in turn creates a larger audience for more media outlets. Potentially there could be an increase in celebrity tabloids' readership. But was there enough gossip to spread around, and were there that many interested readers? The supermarket tabloids were competing for their share of "entertainment junkies."

AMI inaugurated its new image with multi-million-dollar renovations to the former Globe Communications headquarters. An additional fifty million dollars was designated for an aggressive advertising campaign and design updates for the *Enquirer* and the *Star*. The *Star* underwent several transitions in appearance before it ultimately adopted a sleeker magazine look on a glossy-page format with a pastel-pink color theme. The *Enquirer* opted for bright yellow tagged stories, an enlarged, red front page banner, and black-bordered pages. Yet the *Enquirer* was careful not to tamper with its editorial content and style. "The *Enquirer* wasn't about to turn off the 2.2 million readers that make the weekly newspaper the largest in the country . . . we wanted to keep the essence of the *Enquirer*. We're a saucy, bold tabloid," said *Enquirer* editor-in-chief Steve Coz in an interview with the *Palm Beach Post*.

The strategy that AMI employed to sell six supermarket tabloids involved a differentiation of the focus of each tabloid, whereby each would appeal to a broad but distinct group of readers. Instead of duplicating stories and targeting overlapping audiences, each tabloid aimed to define their stories according to readers' preferences and their own editorial expertise. Distinguishing one supermarket tabloid from another is not a clear-cut process, since the essence of the tabloids is a signature style of presentation and tone, and furthermore there is a crossover of similar tabloid themes. Nevertheless, positioning the tabloids so they could carve out their own niche is not an improbable or impracticable idea, as Generoso Pope Jr. discovered when he changed the *National Enquirer*'s focus first to gore and then to the softer supermarket variety mix.

The *Globe* and Tammy Faye Bakker

The six Florida tabloids had a distinctive relationship with their readers that influenced their story coverage. The readers of the *Globe* remembered Tammy Faye Bakker, wife and partner of Jim Bakker, a flamboyant televangelist who enjoyed the extravagant lifestyle provided by a lucrative television ministry active in the mid-1970s. They remembered her bouffant wig, pink lipstick, and long, mascara-heavy eyelashes that glistened with tears as she sang about salvation. To her fans she was a friend who became a victim when her husband had an affair with his church secretary and committed accounting fraud. He went to prison, and the ministry and marriage dissolved.

Tammy Faye did not retire from the public spotlight, and in fact, chronicled her battle with terminal cancer on her website and in televised appearances. There were no extraordinary secrets left to expose, but photographs, as the tabloids are well aware, produce emotions, and emotions sell papers. The *Globe* received a tip that steered reporter Jim McCandlish to a private Mother's Day dinner at a country club in Monroe, North Carolina. The tabloid product was as melodramatic as Tammy Faye's life, "Tammy Faye: Shocking Last Photos, Plus Her Brave Farewell." Haunting, candid photographs showed an emaciated but heroic Tammy Faye, and a heart-rending, sympathetic story described the brave Mother's Day appearance of the "dying Bible Queen." "Tammy Faye's courage was incredible. She always vowed to live her life to the very end—and that's just what she was doing," an inside source told the *Globe*'s readers.

Were these really the last photos? Certainly, when the *Globe* published the photographs on June 4, 2007, it could not foresee when Tammy Faye would die, but readers were satisfied with an emotional send-off for their friend. On July 19, almost seven weeks after the *Globe*'s exclusive, CNN's *Larry King Live* scooped the scoop. Viewed by an audience much larger than the *Globe*'s readership, Tammy Faye granted her final interview on cable television. The following day on July 20, 2007, she passed away.

The *Star* as a Celebrity Magazine

While the *Globe*'s readers marveled at Tammy Faye's amazing eyelashes, perfectly in order despite her terminal illness, the *Star*'s younger readers sought a weekly that would reveal which celebrity was pregnant, had a nose job, or split from his or her spouse. In 2003 the *Star* returned to its roots in New York City to position itself as a competitor with *US Weekly* and *In-Touch* celebrity magazines. The strategy was to repackage the *Star* as a celebrity magazine, a transformation AMI induced by printing it on high-quality, colorful glossy paper, giving it attractively designed pages dominated by photographs, and filling it with the latest celebrity gossip, fashion trends, and lifestyle advice.

To alter the *Star*'s editorial direction, David Pecker hired Bonnie Fuller, former editor at *Glamour*, *Cosmopolitan*, and *US Weekly* and named Advertising Age's Editor of the Year. Briefly, the *Star* considered renouncing cash for tips by building stories from publicist-approved celebrity news. Could the *Star* be both celebrity-friendly and celebrity tell-all? Considering the financial pressure AMI was under and the cutthroat atmosphere of the celebrity publishing business, it was no surprise that the *Star* soon reverted to its tabloid roots to pull in exclusives, expose scandals, and capture attention with outrageous Page One covers described by Fuller as "OMIGOD" covers.

The *Star* was tailored to women under fifty, women who wanted to be entertained by celebrity news. In a 2006 interview with Deborah Solomon of the *New York Times*, Fuller said, "A lot of the traditional women's magazines are too much work. They are full of how-to-service information and that can feel like homework . . . It can make you feel inadequate! When you come home and want to relax, you may not want to read about improving yourself 100 percent. You might want to be satisfied with yourself and have a good laugh looking at what happened to Brad and Angelina this week."

From Liz to Britney

When Larry Haley, assistant executive editor, began working for the *National Enquirer* in 1981, one of his assignments was to monitor the daily activities of actor Liz Taylor in New York City while "Little Foxes" was being shot. Haley, a former crime reporter in Chicago and Miami, followed Liz to restaurants, parties, hotels, and beauty salons. His first solo celebrity page for the *Enquirer* contained a story about a suspected romance between Taylor and her producer.

More than twenty years later in 2003, Haley, on loan from the *Enquirer* to the *Star* during a period when they were short on news editors, led the story about Britney Spears. In 2007 Haley said, "Now at 57, I'm spending every week monitoring the doings of 25-year-old Britney. Not what I envisioned in my old age but hey, she is a pop culture icon and she's what the readers want."

"Britney! She Tells All to *Star*" *Star*™ July 8, 2003.

The first year, 2003, of the *Star*'s official debut as a celebrity magazine, it offered its readers "The Real Britney, Her Life and Her Loves—in Her Own Words." *Star* captured an exclusive interview with popular singer Britney Spears after publishing one of the first stories exposing her party-girl side. Britney denied the article's unflattering portrayal of her, but within a couple of weeks her publicist called the *Star* to arrange a formal interview. Senior reporter David Wright and photo editor Jenny Vega traveled to New York City to produce the kind of story readers expected from the *Star*, "Britney! She Tells All to the *Star*, Boys! Booze! Betrayals! Breakups!"

The *National Enquirer's* Kind of Story

While the *Star* primarily resonated with a younger crowd, the *National Enquirer* appealed to a wide age group of people who expected to be the first to know about the real goings-on in a scandal. The *Enquirer* was not about to abandon what it did well, its trademark investigative reporting, tabloid style. Within a two-month period in 2001, it broke two political scandals of national import.

"Jesse Jackson's Love Child" evolved from a rumor and a tip about an illegitimate child fathered by the Reverend Jesse Jackson, President Bill Clinton's moral advisor and a prominent civil rights leader and activist. At the time, the *Chicago Tribune* also pursued the rumor. "But we went up against dead ends, the same dead ends that the *National Enquirer* ran into. They got past them, and we didn't. Suffice it to say that the *Enquirer* devoted more resources to it than the mainstream media, but it's their kind of story more than it's our kind of story," said *Chicago Tribune* journalist Clarence Page in the *Columbia Journalism Review*.

The *Enquirer*'s kind of scandalous story typically concerns individual guilt or victimization. Frequently, in the process of exposing personal hypocrisy or impropriety, it inflames a public outrage that the mainstream media pursues in depth. Jackson "has been steadfastly meeting his obligations" to the child and her mother, the *Enquirer* reported. The *Enquirer* readers were satisfied. The *Chicago Tribune* readers wanted more answers. In addition to moral accountability, they demanded financial accountability. "Was the severance pay really hush money? Whose money was used to pay for child support or the house? Those questions became relevant after you first establish that this is Jackson's out-of-wedlock child," said Page. The *Chicago Tribune* pursued the story where the *Enquirer* left off.

Whereas reporters followed a rumor in the Jesse Jackson scandal, "Clinton Pardon Payoff Exposed $200,000 Deposited in Secret Family Bank Account" originated from a reporter's curiosity and instinct for a newsworthy story. Senior reporter David Wright actively looked for a potential political scandal in the presidential pardons rushed through at the end of President Clinton's second term. Twelve *Enquirer* reporters were assigned to investigate the pardons, and found the story when they uncovered letters and legal documents that implied the president's brother-in-law, Hugh Rodham, was involved in inappropriate lobbying efforts for pardon pleas. The *Enquirer* produced the bank wire transfer as proof of payment from his clients, though Rodham returned the money under pressure from President Clinton just as the story was about to break. *Newsweek* journalist Michael Isikoff said, "Look, it was a 'slam dunk' story . . . any mainstream news organization, from the *New York Times* to the *Washington Post* to *Newsweek* to CNN would have gone with it in a minute once they had the facts."

In both cases, the *Enquirer* received recognition from the mainstream media for its "rock solid" stories, but a new generation of celebrity-watchers were more interested in the daily activities of glamorous celebrities—people famed for their shocking and often outrageous behavior—than they were in the president's moral advisor or brother-in-law. Whether for an individual owner like Generoso Pope Jr. or a corporate investor like AMI, the expected payback for the additional expenditure of time and money required by investigative reporting is an increase in mass readership. Although the Jesse Jackson and Hugh Rodham stories exhibited the classic elements of a tabloid scandal and achieved credibility, the stories failed to attract a significant new group of readers. Clearly, it was time to focus on the trendy celebrities of the new millennium.

9-11

In 2001 AMI's plans were interrupted by an act of international terrorism. Suddenly, hard news replaced soft celebrity gossip as the heroes and villains of the 9-11 tragedy assumed the role of celebrities themselves. Four hijacked United States passenger planes inflicted grievous damage and massive loss of life when two of them crashed into the Twin Towers of the World Trade Center Complex in New York City, another into the Pentagon in Washington, D.C., and the fourth into a rural field in Pennsylvania. On September 11, 2001, CNN announced on their Web site, "America Under Attack."

Several days later, the first 9-11 cover stories produced by the weekly magazines began to appear. "Sept 11, 2001 the Day That Shook America"(*People*). "One Nation Indivisible" (*Time* magazine). "The Week That Sports Stood Still" (*Sports Illustrated*). And an AMI Special, "The Day That Changed America." Tabloids and mainstream press concurred; God bless America and find Osama bin Laden.

The *Star* paid an emotional tribute to "Our Heroes." The *Globe* speculated, "I Know Where Warlord Lives," and the *Weekly World News*'s Bat Boy enlisted in Marine Corps boot camp to join in the fight against terrorists. But the real story waited to be told in the Middle East: that of the terrorist training camps. Any doubts that the *National Enquirer* had lost its edge were dispelled when "road warrior" reporter Alan Butterfield trekked to the cusp of Khyber Pass in the tribal border region of Afghanistan and Pakistan to interview a former member of one of these camps, producing "The Story Every American Must Read."

Two weeks after the 9-11 attacks Butterfield was on his way to Pakistan. He carried a small camera, a supply of reporter's notebooks, and a satellite phone. He traveled by himself; no military escort, no entourage of photographers, no television crew, and no interpreters.

In the capital city of Islamabad Butterfield lingered at the Marriott Hotel, a hub for foreign journalists, to pick up information. There he found Saeed, a cab driver who owned a car with worn-out shock absorbers, gaps in the floorboard, and of course, no air conditioning. For one hundred U.S. dollars a day Saeed, who spoke several dialects of the native language, became Butterfield's passport to the remote and lawless "Tribal Zone" at Khyber Pass where "the biggest firepower rules."

"*Enquirer* Reporter Puts His Life on the Line Near the Afghan Border" pictured Butterfield in front of a sign that warned, "Foreigners are not allowed beyond this point unless specially permitted by the political agent of the Khyber Agency." Saeed's response, "Don't worry, no problem."

Saeed directed Butterfield to Naseer, a 19-year-old Afghan who escaped from a training camp in the mountains of Afghanistan and fled to a refugee camp of mud huts in Pakistan. Naseer told his own dramatic story, "I was a terrorist soldier for Osama Bin Laden." "Bin Laden Terrorist Tells All" was a first-person interview with no need to resort to "a pal" or "a source" for information. Among his peers, Naseer gained prestige for giving an interview publicized in America, but for his personal safety only his first name was published and his face was obscured. In this instance, the *Enquirer* did not have to tie up its exclusive with a costly contract as it was unlikely Butterfield would lose his story to rival reporters still back in Islamabad.

Over a period of two to three weeks Butterfield spun stories from his travels to Peshawr, near the Khyber Pass, and Gilgit, located to the north alongside the Silk Road near the Chinese border. His stories paired with the *Enquirer's* reports on the status of women in Afghanistan, the Muslim religion, and terrorists in America responded

"Bin Laden Terrorist Tells All" *National Enquirer*™ October 9, 2001.

to what readers wanted at the time: information presented from a personal point of view about a culture and an attack they did not comprehend.

"Bin Laden Terrorist Tells All" was published on October 9, a week after the *Enquirer* issued their first 9-11 cover story on October 2, "Inside the Terrorist Plot, Their Chilling Secret Lives in the U.S." While tabloid readers learned about terrorism abroad, a terror was unleashed close to home upon the AMI headquarters in Boca Raton. Unbeknownst to the staff working to meet deadlines, an anthrax-tainted letter had been delivered to AMI's offices.

The Anthrax Attack on AMI

On October 2, 2001, in Atlantis, Florida, Robert Stevens, photo editor at the *Sun*, was hospitalized at JFK Medical Center with a high fever. Chief of Staff Dr. Larry Bush, a specialist in infectious disease, sent blood samples to a medical research laboratory in Jacksonville. Three days later on Friday, October 5, Stevens, critically infected with pulmonary anthrax, a virulent and rare strain of anthrax bacteria that produces microscopic spores, died. By October 7, another AMI employee, Ernesto Blanco, was hospitalized in Miami. He also was diagnosed, barely in time to receive lifesaving treatment, with pulmonary anthrax. Within hours, the AMI headquarters in Boca Raton was evacuated, sealed from further access, and placed under police guard. The tabloids owned their personal exclusive, "Bio-Terrorism, the Florida Anthrax Attack on *Enquirer* Headquarters."

The seventh of October was a Sunday, but the AMI building did not stand empty. CEO David Pecker was meeting with his administrative staff, and several editors and writers were working in their offices on stories for Monday, the lockup day when the final copy was sent to the presses. Late in the afternoon, the Federal Bureau of Investigation ordered Pecker and his staff to immediately drop what they were doing and evacuate the building. Preliminary swab samples, collected

"Bio-Terrorism" *National Enquirer*™ October 30, 2001.

by a team from the Centers for Disease Control, the FBI, and the United States Postal Service, showed positive results for anthrax both on Stevens' computer keyboard and in the mailroom. By Monday, the AMI offices were quarantined. Over time, traces of anthrax spores, believed to have been disseminated through anthrax-tainted letters, were found in more than eighty locations inside the three-story, sixty thousand square foot AMI building.

Everyone who might have been in the building since the first of August reported to the Palm Beach County Health Department Office in Delray Beach for testing and to receive a 60-day supply of the antibiotic Cipro. This included the entire AMI staff, their families, and even David Perel's red teacup poodle, Scooby Doo, the recipient of an exclusive, "The Little Dog Who's Licking Terrorism." "The puppy had spent about two hours at American Media," the *National Enquirer* informed their readers. "While roaming around the office, Scooby Doo had even ventured down a hall to the *Sun* newspaper offices and was sniffing around some of the desks—including the desk of Robert Stevens, who later tragically died of anthrax."

"Evacuated. Medicated. Dedicated." In a message to the readers "from the people who lived through the nightmare," *Enquirer* editor-in-chief David Perel wrote, "We Will Not Yield to Fear." "Locked out of our own building, we created makeshift headquarters in two cramped locations, and working elbow-to-elbow in conditions one person termed a 'tabloid sweatshop' we put out the newspaper. Worried about our families, our children, our co-workers, ourselves, we worked deep into the night, refusing the opportunity to go home until our jobs were done." Working feverishly on their various publications, AMI's employees produced on time their weekly share of tabloid entertainment.

CEO David Pecker appeared on CNN's *Larry King Live* to assure the public, "There is no risk of exposure of anthrax being transmitted by handling any tabloids or any publications published by American Media." As additional reassurance, a banner reading "This Paper Not

Bob Stevens

Tabloids are accustomed to receiving unusual reader responses to their stories, but one particular letter, addressed to Jennifer Lopez, care of the *Sun*, intrigued photo editor Bob Stevens. "It was a business-size sheet of stationary decorated with pink and blue clouds around the edges. It was folded into three sections, and in the middle was a pile of what looked like pink-tinged talcum powder. Sticking out of the powder was a little gold something, I couldn't tell what," said photo assistant Roz Suss in "The Nightmare That Came in the Mail." Some hypothesize that this letter was the anthrax-tainted one and Stevens, his eyesight poor, leaned close to examine the powder and thereby inhaled some of its fine particles. However he was exposed, Stevens became the first fatality of the post–9-11 anthrax attack on AMI headquarters.

Bob Stevens was recruited from England to work as a photo enhancer for the *Enquirer* shortly after it was moved to Lantana, Florida, in 1971. "He had the eye," said Tom Wilbur, former managing editor of the *National Examiner*. "He was the best retoucher in the USA." His most famous work of art was the transformation of a dark, fuzzy photograph of Elvis Presley in his coffin into a recognizable image. As technology improved, Stevens substituted the computer for the air brush.

Three times Stevens retired from one or another of the tabloids. Three times his friends hosted a going-away party. Six months prior to the anthrax attack, he returned to the *Sun* as photo editor.

Stevens is remembered for his kindness and humor. "My favorite Bob Stevens line was this," said Rick Harlowe, former photo editor at the *Globe*. At the entrance to the Globe Communications building was a large statue of Atlas—rumored to have originally been placed in front of a gym—carrying a golden globe on his back. Harlowe initiated a top ten list for "Best Names for the Statue." Stevens "won hands down," said Harlowe. "And there was no sense of even asking for nine other suggestions. Bob's contribution—Tab Lloyd."

Printed in the State of Florida" ran across the top of the front page of each of the tabloids. In spite of these measures, a panicked public bought 15 percent fewer tabloids than was normal at the time, a trend that persisted for several months.

A temporary quarantine for the AMI building stretched out into a permanence that threatened the future of Florida's supermarket tabloids. A chain-link fence was installed around the building and security guards patrolled the grounds on a 24-hour circuit. For months that stretched into years, FBI agents and bioterrorism response teams in protective suits and masks entered the deserted AMI headquarters, now known as the anthrax building, to search for clues and swab desks, letters, and air-conditioning filters. The United States Justice Department guaranteed in writing that their investigators would not

---

Left Behind

"I never, never dreamed at all we'd never be able to get back in the building," said AMI's CEO David Pecker in an interview with Eliot Kleinberg of the *Palm Beach Post*. While the FBI conducted their investigation, everything inside the building remained exactly as it was left on October 7, 2001. Pecker's car keys lay on his desk, and $50,000 in cash was locked in the safe. Mike Nevard's cardigan from his days as a Fleet Street reporter was draped over the back of his chair. Family photographs, a first edition book by Ernest Hemingway, Ray Villwock's rolodex, filled with irreplaceable phone numbers, and Joe West's Three Stooges coffee mug were contaminated and could never be retrieved. Left behind in David Perel's office were a painting by his daughter and memorabilia from the O. J. Simpson investigation.

Among the archives in the phenomenal tabloid library were several million photographs of all the celebrities—Liz Taylor, Rock Hudson, Elvis Presley, Madonna—that made tabloid headlines. Abandoned albums contained decades' worth of story clippings, and bound volumes preserved front page covers. All were destined to exist in a state of limbo and decay while the fate of the AMI building and its contents was decided.

The "anthrax" building with chain-link fence. (Courtesy of Tom Wilbur.)

read or remove the tabloids' crucial private files and lists of confidential informants. In the meantime, AMI settled into leased office space across the road in the T-Rex Corporate Center.

Nationally, AMI's crisis alerted the nation to a real threat and may have thus saved lives. Within the close-knit tabloid community, the death of a friend and colleague was a personal tragedy, while the building's contamination dealt a serious economic blow to AMI. By 2002, the vacant AMI building's value had declined from $4.7 million in 2001 to $1.7 million. AMI spent about $50,000 on security for the building, and efforts to enlist federal aid to help pay the estimated $5 million cleanup costs failed. In 2003, having sustained a $10 million real estate loss in addition to sacrificing a treasure trove of original photographs, AMI sold the still-quarantined building and its contents for $40,000 to a Boca Raton real estate developer. Decontamination, a costly and laborious process involving the circulation of chlorine dioxide gas through the air conditioning and heating systems, began in July 2004 and concluded in February 2007. In May of 2007, a credit card company bought the building for $10 million, a price well below its value because of the stigma attached to it. The boxes of individually-treated photographs were believed to have remained in the possession of the seller. Seven years after the anthrax attack on AMI, a bio-defense researcher and prime suspect in the case (which later also involved similar attacks upon the United States Congress and a network broadcasting company) apparently committed suicide before charges were filed against him, leaving loose ends in the case.

Tabloid Valley Moves On

The memories of the anthrax incident will not disappear for AMI, but in 2003 it moved on with its business and set out to revitalize the supermarket tabloid industry. The *Star* held onto its position as AMI's entry into the expanding celebrity magazine market and the other five tabloids concentrated on delivering more tabloid content than the mainstream media could. In 2003 the *Enquirer* was the first to report, "Rush Limbaugh Caught in Drug Ring . . . Exclusive Interview: His Drug Supplier Tells All," and in 2006, "O. J. Confesses in Tell-All Book" scored a major coup as the first story to break the book's existence.

The Troubled Tabloids

In 2005, in an effort to infuse the *National Enquirer* with fresh energy, David Pecker moved its newsroom to New York City and staffed it with a newly arrived influx of twenty-two Fleet Streeters. Apparently, the Brit's choice of editorial content—revolving around naughty scandals, drug dens, and sex rings—did not please the American supermarket buyers, because circulation sales dropped. A year later Pecker announced, "The company wants to save money." The Fleet Streeters departed to London, the *Enquirer* returned to Boca Raton, and David Perel became editor-in-chief.

A Bigger Story

Occasionally, a big story is dropped for one even bigger. In 2007, *National Enquirer* senior reporter David Wright was in Houston, Texas, covering the story of a woman astronaut charged with the attempted kidnapping of her romantic rival. Unexpectedly and mysteriously, former Playboy model and tabloid celebrity Anna Nicole Smith died at the Seminole Hard Rock Hotel and Casino in Hollywood, Florida. Wright immediately booked a flight from Houston to Nassau, where Anna Nicole's home in the Bahamas was located, bypassing Florida and the daily press conferences altogether. "We cover stories differently than everyone else. We don't go to press conferences because it's a public arena for ideas and news. The *National Enquirer* is interested in what is not common knowledge," explained Wright.

Wright had sources in Nassau, cultivated when he covered the story of the death of Anna Nicole's son. They supplied information about what went on inside Anna Nicole's mansion and gave details about her intimate relationships. "It was just one of those rare situations where we're covering one big story and an even bigger one comes up, and I just happened to be the reporter with the key Bahamas contacts," said Wright. Ultimately, the *Enquirer* hired a freelancer to produce the story about the astronaut.

In March 2007, the *Palm Beach Post* reported, "AMI Bleeds $160 Million." New York publishing consultant Martin Walker said in an interview with journalist Jeff Ostrowski, "They were heavily leveraged and in debt to begin with. Newsstand sales in general were down across the board for magazines. And you can get the salacious stuff on the Internet. It's a confluence of a lot of things." In the second half of 2006, even sales of the stalwart *Readers Digest* were off 12.2 percent, while the *Star*'s newsstand circulation sales, the ones that generate the greatest income, dropped to an all-time low of 560,000 copies. Undoubtedly, in spite of modest rebounds in 2007 of single-

"Anna Nicole Death Scene Photos" *National Enquirer*™ February 26, 2007.

copy sales for the *Star* and the *Enquirer*, the supermarket tabloids were in trouble. This was going on even as AMI initiated cost-cutting actions which trimmed down the size of *Country Weekly* and *Men's Fitness* and printed *Shape* on lighter paper stock. Additional cost-cutting measures precipitated the closure of three other publications—including AMI's Wal-Mart magazine, *Looking Good Now*—and the elimination of numerous jobs. In 2007 AMI reportedly carried more than one million dollars in debt and was rumored to be seeking a merger partner.

Ultimately, it was the fantastically creative *Weekly World News* that lost the numbers game. In the 1980s a million people read "Elvis Is Alive," but by 2007 fewer than ninety thousand wanted to know about the escapades of Bat Boy.

Chapter 9

The Future of Tabloid Valley

ON JULY 24, 2007, AMI abandoned the print version of the zaniest of its tabloids, the *Weekly World News*. On July 25, an e-mail circulated throughout the tabloid community: "Time for a Wake—Our Deceased—the *Weekly World News*. Spread the word among the tabloid community." Tabloid colleagues and friends gathered to mourn the past, celebrate the present, and ponder the uncertain future of the once-indomitable supermarket tabloids. The *Weekly World News* was the first casualty among the six original American supermarket tabloids, the first to succumb to dismal circulation sales and a fading appeal. But even the *National Enquirer*, the superstar of Tabloid Valley, was not immune to the forces that threatened not only an individual publication, but the very format that defined supermarket tabloids. Sometime between the heyday of Tabloid Valley in the 1970s and the new millennium, television, the Internet, and slick celebrity magazines siphoned off the exuberance of tabloid storytelling and made what had traditionally been tabloids' subject matter their domain, leaving supermarket tabloids with outdated spoofs and what were often upstaged celebrity exclusives.

Originally, the supermarket tabloids branded themselves the publication of choice for irreverent or lighthearted entertainment. "We're fun, we're fascinating," said Billy Burt, former editor and reporter for the *National Enquirer* and the *National Examiner*. "When you don't

"Half-Human Half-Fish Are Washing Up in Florida" *Weekly World News*™ June 3, 1997.

want to be bored, you turn to your tabloid . . . We're providing them (the readers) with an alternative, relieving them from the barrage of boredom that hits them every day. The magazines that scoff at us, like *People* magazine, like *US* magazine, they're doing exactly what we're doing, only they're trying to disguise it. We yell it, they whisper it." He was wrong; by the end of the '90s—the "tabloid decade"—everyone was yelling it.

The Old Guard

On March 19, 2007, William "Billy" Alexander Burt, "loved as a wit and raconteur," died in Atlantis, Florida. Four days later, friends and family gathered to celebrate his life and the passing of an era with a wake at Brogues Pub in Lake Worth. Three hours into the wake, a black limousine approached on Lake Avenue and parked in front of Brogues. Florida governor Charlie Crist joined Burt's family to raise a toast to one of Tabloid Valley's most legendary journalists.

Billy Burt, a Fleet Streeter from Scotland, was recruited by former editor-in-chief Iain Calder to work at the *Enquirer* in the early 1970s. "He was one of the most colorful journalists I've ever met," said Calder in a *Palm Beach Post* interview. "As a reporter, if there was a wall, then he'd try to climb over, and if he couldn't climb over, he'd run through it. He was totally full of energy, and the closest thing to a Scottish leprechaun you could ever get." Burt was the perfect candidate to send to Peru to track down a Uruguayan rugby team who had survived following a plane crash in the Andes Mountains by eating the bodies of their dead teammates. Once the survivors were discovered, a snowstorm prevented the rescue team from airlifting them out of the mountains, but there was a story to tell, and the *Enquirer* went after it. Burt, the "wee Scot," trekked through the rugged terrain to the wreckage and was the first to take down the uncensored interview of the sixteen survivors—cannibals, if you read the tabloids—for a classic *Enquirer* story.

Those were the early days of the *Enquirer* in Lantana, characterized by the heady business of building a new product, the supermarket tabloid. Inspired tabloid journalists chased UFO's and medical cures and crashed celebrity weddings and funerals. They were the *Enquirer*'s "wild bunch." What recruit, certainly not Jim McCandlish, could resist Billy Burt's sales pitch for the *Enquirer*? "I'm working for this crazy outfit in Florida where you get to do the best stories for great money. They get you your Green Card, pay unlimited expenses, send you all over the world. You stay in the best hotels and eat in the finest restaurants. And you live next to the ocean in South Florida. You can't beat it with a stick!"

Surely, Tabloid Valley will fondly remember Burt and his colleagues, who were part of the creative news-making team of Tabloid Valley, but by 2000, the once-dominant Florida tabloids that packed the supermarket checkout counter racks jostled for position in a crowded celebrity media marketplace, and the tales of intrepid reporters who spent months working on intriguing stories in far-off parts of the world, meanwhile accumulating paychecks so fast they went untouched for weeks, were brilliant memories of the past.

Where do the supermarket tabloids go from here? Stressed by financial and editorial pressures, AMI made choices. It retained the print *Globe*, *National Examiner*, and *Sun* for a dwindling readership that resisted transitioning to Internet media. The majority of the company's resources went to the *National Enquirer* and the *Star*, AMI's two top sellers of celebrity news. The *Star*, from its inception gossipy and girly, and the *Enquirer*, while not exactly hip, relevant to a wide range of readers, relaunched their Internet sites with online exclusives and user message boards in an effort to reach a new audience. While the tabloids transitioned to the Internet, they gambled on the staying power, at least for a short time, of the print version, which brought in revenue from circulation sales, the industry's traditional mainstay. A diminished but still active core of investigative reporters tracked

Heath & Mary-Kate
WHAT SHE'S HIDING

Star

WORLD EXCLUSIVE

YES IT'S TRUE!

Angie's Pregnant — With TWINS!

$3.49 US / $4.79 CANADA

FEBRUARY 11, 2008

Angie's secret four-month in vitro ordeal

The night she told Brad: WE DID IT!

"Yes It's True" *Star*™ February 11, 2008.

"Stars With Cellulite" *National Enquirer*™ January 15, 2007.

down stories of autopsy photos, a secret pregnancy, or a 14-day marriage of a pop culture star.

The Glossy *Star*

Any celebrity-watchers who logged onto the *Star*'s Internet site on January 24, 2008, were the first to know that Hollywood A-list couple Angelina Jolie and Brad Pitt were expecting twin babies. Unable to hold on to the news in the competitive gossip business, the *Star* announced its scoop on the web. A week later it matched its web posting with a longer, detailed version of the story in its print issue, "Yes It's True! Angie's Pregnant—with Twins!"

The *Star* delivered its scoop wrapped in a glossy, photo-oriented page format designed to attract the younger female audience who wanted a dressed-up tabloid. Did glossy make a difference? One reason the supermarket tabloids were successful was that they dished up the dirt better than anyone else at the time. The *Star* was certainly good at that, but as a glossy magazine, it was just one of many, and it would have to out-gossip the rest of the pack.

The New Face of the *National Enquirer*

The *National Enquirer* retained a modicum of human interest stories, "Woman Falls off Mountain—and Lives to Tell about It!" and sensational crime stories, "Juror's Secret Letters Grounds to Reopen Case," to please their longtime readers, but the highest priority was to attract a new generation of consumers. To jumpstart the highly visible presence of the *Enquirer* on the hot celebrity scene in 2007, AMI created the position of entertainment editor, based out of Manhattan, to present the public face of the *Enquirer*. Dorothy Cascerceri, a journalism graduate of George Washington University, made appearances at celebrity publicity events, gossiped with television journalist Geraldo Rivera on *Geraldo At Large*, participated in radio call-ins, and conducted one-on-one publicist-arranged interviews. She was there for the *Enquirer* at Malibu parties, the Soho, New York City, apartment of an actor who was the victim of a fatal accident, and VH1's Save the Music Foundation 10th Anniversary Gala.

On September 20, 2007, pop diva Mariah Carey was an honoree at VH1's Save the Music Foundation Gala, a red-carpet affair held in New York City to honor the musicians and politicians who support the music programs VH1 provides in public schools. Lined up along the aisle enclosing the red carpet, photographers were assigned to one side, the television reporters and camera crews were amassed on the opposite side, and at the far end, deemed a low priority, were reporters representing about a dozen members of the print media, including the *Enquirer*. As Mariah, bedecked in a stunning purple gown, reached the end of her stroll along the red carpet, the newspaper and magazine reporters were divided into two groups, and each group was allotted one question restricted to the music gala, Carey's perfume line, or her recent album. But the *Enquirer's* readers wanted gossipy stories—what was going on in Mariah's life, who was her trainer, what was she eating, and what advice did she give for women who wanted a svelte figure?

The old guard reporters of the *Enquirer* would have been proud of how Ms. Cascerceri ignored the rules, jumped right in, and asked the question everybody wanted to know—what was the "Secret of Hot New Body?" "A bleak diet," the singer responded, but she also credited her success to discipline and a skilled personal trainer. Of course, in the public venue of the press conference, the *Enquirer* had to share its interview with the rest of the reporters, which meant it appeared on www.People.com and all throughout television and the Internet. Probably only the reporters at the event knew who initially hooked the exclusive interview. Was the exclusive, printed two weeks later, still of value for the *Enquirer*? The *Enquirer* placed its faith in understanding its readers. The story they told spoke to the audience with a "va-va-voom" photo, purchased from one of the celebrity photographers, and an inspirational story that carried a special message from Mariah: "I'm not supposed to be a stick-figure kind of girl."

The Tabloid Challenge

Tabloids, in one form or another, have existed for several hundred years. How will the supermarket tabloids survive in an era during which they must compete with the Internet and cable television, where scandals and celebrity news are available instantly, any time of the day or night?

The *National Enquirer*, the *Star*, and the *Globe* were betting that their experience following rumors and digging for stories would keep them in the celebrity game. "Of course, a print magazine can't beat an online site for speed . . . but it can still go out and find its own exclusive stories and pictures," said Steven LeGrice, former executive editor of the *Star*. "It has always been the big stories that brought in the readers. Unfortunately at the moment the magazines seem content to repackage the same stories you can read online." Undoubtedly, the time lapse between when news appears online and in print influences the relevance of a story and makes it necessary for a weekly tabloid to find an original and compelling angle. Flooded by scoops that are widely circulated within minutes, the consumer wants a story that adds up to something more than just an unfounded rumor. The pride and success of the supermarket tabloids had been to understand what made a compelling story, but today a changed playing field is challenging their ability to do this. "The same stories are now covered by celebrity gossip magazines and TV shows, the Internet (where gossip can travel much faster), and regular newspapers, all of which now tend to feature celebrity news and multiple human interest stories," said anthropologist S. Elizabeth Bird. "The boundaries of what is acceptable, in terms of explicit material, have been pushed back significantly across the board." Beating the mainstream competition became far more difficult for tabloids when their competition joined them.

In fact, supermarket tabloids were so successful with their product that their style permeated and shaped a tabloid culture that voided the uniqueness of its originator. Capitalizing on the tabloids' popularity, tabloid television, followed by Internet gossip sites, adopted eye-catching graphics, an emotional tone, and similar editorial choices. "There's no way the tabs can compete with the Internet or TV," said Phil Bunton, former executive editor of the *Star* and editor-in-chief of Globe Communications. "TV has bigger pockets and can get on the air immediately." Historically, the supermarket tabloids quickly dealt with the competition through innovation and adaptations, skills requisite for success in a free enterprise system. But as far back as the 1980s they missed the opportunity to attack the television field as they had blitzed the supermarket outlets. Rather belatedly, they were drawn to the Internet, where advertising sales and readers gravitating from the online to the print version were expected to generate revenue.

"Tabloids will survive, but will we be able to recognize them?" asked Steven LeGrice. Increasingly, technological advances influence in what form the public gets their tabloid news. "People want to SEE things NOW. I think the Internet will kill tabloids—except—tabloid newspapers will become tabloid blogs—so you get all your juicy gossip online," said Malcolm Balfour, former associate editor at the *National Enquirer*. A mindboggling multimedia landscape has the capacity to instantly deliver the tabloid scoop on a portable computer or a cell phone with web services, interactive video, and television, and more is yet to come technologically. "Inevitably tabloids will evolve into a higher technological form; the words will no longer be ink on paper and they will most certainly be delivered in some electronic form but the content will still be 'tabloid,'" said David Perel, *National Enquirer*'s editor-in-chief and AMI's director of editorial content. "The only way tabloid publications will survive is by adapting to this reality and changing their physical form."

Without a doubt, the primary subject of the supermarket tabloids, gossip, is as popular as ever. "The reports of tabloids' death are greatly exaggerated given our age-old fascination with gossip—in this case, about celebrities," said Steven Edwards, former *Star* reporter. But the medium, the tabloid format that carries the message, is in danger of extinction, of becoming a news museum exhibit. "People may, however, come to regard them more as a coffee-table accessory than a source of the latest developments," said Edwards. To the detriment of the supermarket tabloids, the speed and accessibility of the Internet and television have changed our ways to get news. People who were standoffish to the tabloids in the supermarkets now can get the scoop on celebrities while in the privacy of their home by watching television or surfing the Internet. They can receive their gossip in small bites, updated several times a day on the Internet, and enjoy interactive features such as message boards. It is much like the "old days" when friends kept updated by phone—"did you hear the latest?" They can choose www.gawker.com for "media gossip and pop culture round the clock," or "celebrity, sex, fashion without airbrushing" on www.jezebel.com. TMZ, cited by *Time* magazine as one of the "coolest websites" in 2006, covers entertainment news on the Internet and television. Why then should one buy a tabloid at the supermarket? Apparently, there is a large mass of consumers who do not buy them; from the early 1990s to present, the overall sales of supermarket tabloids have been on a consistent decline. It is not likely to reverse.

"Competition for time and attention is more than fierce, and electronic delivery is easier than ever to access," said Mike Foley, journalism professor at the University of Florida. "Can the tabs get more outrageous? Can they compete with YouTube videos of drunk or half-naked celebrities? Will people look at them when they're not waiting in the grocery checkout line? I think it's doubtful." The YouTube and MySpace generation "reads" the Internet and television instead of a newspaper or book. They do not stand in the grocery store checkout

Acknowledgments

THOUGH MY SOURCES are listed throughout the text and the biblio-graphic essay, my especial gratitude to all of the tabloid journalists that trusted me to tell their stories warrants this more personal, redundant mention of their names. I could not have written this book without them. They went out of their way to accommodate my research and welcomed me into the tabloid community. From storage units, ga-rages, cramped offices, and even a daughter's home in England, they retrieved the original issues containing their stories. When I needed an important photograph, Tom Wilbur produced one ready for pub-lication. When I needed a place to stay, Jim McCandlish offered his apartment. Thank you, Jack Alexander, Malcolm Balfour, Bill Bates, Phil Bunton, Alan Butterfield, Iain Calder, Dorothy Cascerceri, Morag Dick, Steven Edwards, Joanna Elm, Al Fayette, John Garton, Barney Giambalvo, Jay Gourley, Larry Haley, Rick Harlowe, John Harris, Lee Harrison, Sal Ivone, Dick Kaplan, Jim Leggett, Steven LeGrice, Jim McCandlish, Mike Nevard, David Perel, Bob Temmey, Candace Trunzo, Ray Villwock, Joe West, Emily Hamer-West, Tom Wilbur, and David Wright.

I am especially indebted to David Perel, *National Enquirer*'s editor-in-chief, who invited me to the AMI newsroom, where the future of the supermarket tabloids is being played out. Anytime, any day, Logan Perel, AMI research associate, provided valuable assistance.

Thank you, John Byram, editor-in-chief at the University Press of Florida, for suggesting the topic of *Tabloid Valley*, and also for placing your faith in me. Always, you generously shared your expertise and provided encouragement. I would also like to extend my thanks to Michele Fiyak-Burkley, my UPF project editor, and Corey Brady, my copy editor, for their worthy contributions to this endeavor.

I am fortunate to have good friends, especially Jeanne Buckingham and Otto Tomasch, Don Burkins and Brigitte Krause, and Mimi and George Noppenberger, longtime friends from Pennsylvania and Maryland who are my enthusiastic cheerleaders. In Florida, Eden and Marc Cross, Maxine Kronich, and Marisella Veiga have always been there for me during this long venture.

Special thanks to my amazing daughters, Bridget and Jessica, and their families. Thank you, Barry, my soul mate, for sharing the laughter and tears that go into creating a book.

Bibliographic Essay

I began my research at the New York City Public Library viewing on microfiche the predecessors of the supermarket tabloids: the nineteenth-century penny papers, the *New York World* and the *New York Journal*, who were accused of yellow journalism, and the picture newspapers: the *Graphic*, the *New York Daily News*, and the *New York Daily Mirror*. Although the New York Public Library does not have a complete collection of the print supermarket tabloids, I was able to sample representative early editions of the *New York Enquirer*, the *National Enquirer*, and the *Star* to appreciate their flavor.

My research continued at the University of Florida Journalism Library. Assisted by Associate University Librarian Patrick Reakes, I accessed archived news clips from newspapers and magazines. My main newspaper sources were the *New York Times*, *Washington Post*, *Wall Street Journal*, *Miami Herald*, and *Palm Beach Post*. I also retrieved news clips from a search engine on my personal computer.

The reference books detailing the history of American newspaper journalism that I utilized included *Jazz Journalism* by Simon Michael Bessie, *Main Currents in the History of American Journalism* by Willard Grosvenor Bleyer, and *Discovering the News: A Social History of American Newspapers* by Michael Schudson. Especially, *The Untold Story* by Iain Calder, *I Watched a Wild Hog Eat My Baby* by Bill Sloan, and *For Enquiring Minds* by S. Elizabeth Bird provided valuable background information about tabloid journalism. A complete list of the reference books used appears in the bibliography.

Material regarding Florida's history, flavor, and culture was derived from my own experiences, the University of Florida History Library, and interviews with Lantana Town Manager Mike Bornstein, Jack Carpenter of the Lantana Historical Society, Gary Hines at the Business Development Board of Palm Beach County, and Attorney Harvey Oyer.

Midway through completing my manuscript, I was fortunate enough to spend time in the AMI newsroom, home to the supermarket tabloids in Boca Raton, Florida. David Perel, editor-in-chief of the *National Enquirer* and director of editorial content for AMI, shared his experiences as reporter and editor, and helped me to understand the world of the supermarket tabloids. When I needed to verify information or locate a copy of one of the tabloid stories that figure predominately in this book, Logan Perel, Stephanie Keiper, and Alison Rayman from the AMI Research Department were there to help. Although the anthrax contamination of AMI's headquarters resulted in the loss of its extensive library dating back to the first issue of the *National Enquirer*, a portion of this historical collection is either safe in a warehouse or stored in computer files as digitized copies which AMI was in the process of archiving when its print library was contaminated.

Among the journalists I consulted are Mike Foley, a prominent member of the College of Journalism and Communications at the University of Florida, Roy Peter Clark of the Poynter Institute of Journalism, and Jeff Klinkenberg of the *St. Petersburg Times*.

The heart of this book is derived from the detailed recollections and insights—generously shared with me during many interviews, phone calls, and e-mails—of the supermarket tabloids' reporters and editors. Tabloid journalists are fun, intelligent, and skilled at what they do—dig up and tell good stories. In particular, Jack Alexander, Malcolm Balfour, Bill Bates, Phil Bunton, Alan Butterfield, Iain Calder, Dorothy Cascerceri, Morag Dick, Steven Edwards, Joanna Elm, Al Fayette, John Garton, Barney Giambalvo, Jay Gourley, Larry Haley, Rick Harlowe, John Harris, Lee Harrison, Sal Ivone, Dick Kaplan, Jim Leggett, Steven LeGrice, Jim McCandlish, Mike Nevard, David Perel, Bob Temmey, Candace Trunzo, Joe West, Emily Hamer-West, Tom Wilbur, and David Wright are an integral part of this story of Tabloid Valley.

Prologue: Who Mourns for the *Weekly World News*?

The quote from actor and writer John Waters is taken from his book, *Crackpot!* The quote from actor Jerry Seinfeld can be found at www.brainyquote.com.

"The most creative newspaper": Peter Carlson, "All the News That Seemed Unfit to Print," *Washington Post*, August 7, 2007.

"Welcome, tabloid brothers and sisters": Jim McCandlish, speaking at the *Weekly World News*'s wake, September 2, 2007.

Eddie Clontz's obituary: *The Economist*, February 19, 2004.

AMI's announcement of the *Weekly World News*'s closure: Lori Becker, "*Weekly World News* Tabloid to Close Up Shop," *Palm Beach Post*, July 24, 2007.

"Our only limit was YOUR imagination": Joe West, in an e-mail sent on December 5, 2007.

Chapter 1. A Small Pill, Easy to Swallow

Definition of a "tabloid": Webster's New Twentieth Century Dictionary, unabridged second edition, p. 1855.

Observations about the tabloid's style and format, and "the size of the container": Roy Peter Clark, in an interview on August 29, 2006.

Personality of tabloids: Sal Ivone, in a phone interview on October 15, 2007.

"A story that the reader": Phil Bunton, in an e-mail sent on July 21, 2007.

"Picture form": Bill Bates, in an interview on November 6, 2006.

"Money quote": John Garton, in an interview on June 9, 2007.

"He's Going to Kill Me": John Blosser, Michael Glynn, and John South, "The O. J. Murders," *National Enquirer*, June 28, 1994.

"Memorandum, Generoso Pope Jr. to Editorial Staff": sent August 17, 1973.

Information for "A Tabloid Story": Jay Gourley, in a phone interview on July 2, 2007 and in an e-mail on August 20, 2007.

"Probably would not" and "It was an important": Jay Gourley in an e-mail on August 20, 2007.

Kissinger: "Rubbish Analysis": James Parcell, *Washington Post*, July 21, 1975.

"We didn't have to make it up": Joanna Elm, in an interview on June 23, 2007.

"Suspect" checkbook journalism: Jack Doppelt, in a PBS interview on January 26, 2004, accessible at www.pbs.org/newshour.

Checkbook journalism "as a tool": David Perel, in an interview on June 12, 2007.

"Reporter's edge": Steven Edwards, in an interview on March 25, 2007.

Ruth Annan, "we police the copy," and Elizabeth Bird, "accurate quotes": S. Elizabeth Bird, *For Enquiring Minds*, pp. 93–94.

Time's fact-checking system: Norberto Angletti and Alberto Oliva, *Magazines That Make History*, p. 32.

"That's exactly what was going through my mind": Jim McCandlish, in an e-mail sent on December 16, 2007.

Information and quotes for "The Tabloid Photographer" and "The Paparazzi": Jim Leggett, in phone interviews conducted and e-mails sent on September 13 and October 14, 16, and 17, 2007.

"Finding ourselves in danger": Jim Leggett, in an e-mail sent on October 17, 2007.

"But although tabloids": S. Elizabeth Bird, *For Enquiring Minds*, p. 8.

Helen Jewett: Willard Grosvenor Bleyer, *Main Currents in the History of American Journalism*, p. 193.

"Yellow Journalism": S. Elizabeth Bird, *For Enquiring Minds*, pp. 16–18, and Simon Michael Bessie, *Jazz Journalism*, p. 55.

New York Graphic and "Composographs": Frank Mallen, *Sauce For the Gander*. Insert: "Composite Gallery."

DEAD!: *New York Daily News*, April 12, 1936, on microfiche at the New York City Public Library.

New York Daily Mirror: Simon Michael Bessie, *Jazz Journalism*, p. 147.

"A dumping ground": Generoso Pope Jr. in an interview with William R. Amlong, "Pope: The High Priest of Lowbrow," *Miami Herald*, January 14, 1973.

"It would not become a tabloid": Generoso Pope Jr., in an interview for the *New York Times*, April 4, 1952.

Chapter 2. The Man and His Vision

"In an age darkened": *New York Enquirer*, April 7, 1952, and "The Man Behind the *Enquirer*," *Washington Post*, April 2, 1978.

"Scurrility" of *Confidential*: "Success in the Sewer," *Time* magazine, July 11, 1955.

First issue of the *New York Enquirer*: William R. Amlong, "Pope: The High Priest of Lowbrow," *Miami Herald*, January 14, 1973.

"Fed up with government bureaucracy": ibid.

Loan for the purchase of the *New York Enquirer*: Iain Calder, *The Untold Story*, p. 31.

Letters to the Editor: *New York Enquirer*, January 26 and March 8, 1953.

"If it was blood that interested people, I'd give it to them": "Goodbye To Gore," *Time* magazine, February 21, 1972.

"It bothered the hell out of me running that kind of paper": William R. Amlong, "Pope: The High Priest of Lowbrow," *Miami Herald*, January 14, 1973.

"The Duchess" Virginia Marmaduke: Larry Haley, in an interview on July 17, 2007.

Marmaduke obituary: Brenda Warner Rotzoll, "Virginia Marmaduke; Pioneering Reporter," *Chicago Sun Times*, November 11, 2001.

"Newspapering won't make you a millionaire": K.C. Jaehnig, "The Duchess Virginia Marmaduke Dead at 93," *Southern Windows*, Southern Illinois University, November 21, 2001.

Nevada State Journal, Sonja McCaskie: Joyce M. Cox, Head of Reference Services at the Nevada State Library and Archives.

"Then gore covered the page": Barney Giambalvo, in an interview on September 3, 2007.

Information for the Clark Gable story and "No problem": Bill Bates, in an interview on November 6, 2006.

Information about *Midnight*: Bill Sloan, *I Watched A Wild Hog Eat My Baby*, p. 62.

Distribution Services Inc.: Devin Leonard, "The Tabloid King's Dilemma," *Fortune*, November 1, 2004.

"I knew we had to change": Malcolm Balfour, "*Enquirer*: Violence Gets the Ax," *Washington Post*, October 15, 1972.

"If *News of the World* can sell": Bill Sloan, *I Watched A Wild Hog Eat My Baby*, p. 38.

"Genius at anticipating": Jim McCandlish, in an interview on September 23, 2006.

Joseph Sorrentino quote: Bill Sloan, *I Watched A Wild Hog Eat My Baby*, p. 79.

"Pope did what no one else had done": Malcolm Balfour, in an interview on September 23, 2006.

"Lucky Dog" Christmas story: Bob Temmey, in a phone interview and an e-mail on October 17, 2007.

Chapter 3. Welcome to Florida, Welcome to the *National Enquirer*

"We couldn't function properly": Malcolm Balfour, "*Enquirer*: Violence Gets the Ax," *Washington Post*, October 15, 1972.

National Enquirer's landscaped grounds: Paul Bannister, www.gentlemanranters.com, August 13, 2007.

"Pope insisted": Barney Giambalvo, in an interview on September 3, 2007.

"Anybody who can't tell": Bill Sloan, *I Watched A Wild Hog Eat My Baby*, p. 110.

"The Old Royal Typewriter": Larry Haley, in an e-mail sent on July 17, 2007.

"Story angle": Iain Calder, in a phone interview on January 10, 2007.

"Entertain, inform": ibid.

"Constantly think": "Memorandum, Generoso Pope Jr. to Editorial Staff," sent August 17, 1973.

"Empowered its readers": Iain Calder, in a phone interview on January 10, 2007.

"Why I Love America": Malcolm Balfour, in an interview on September 23, 2006.

Pope's guiding principles: ibid.

"Two best reporters": ibid.

Rating system: based upon interviews with Iain Calder, John Harris, Jim McCandlish, and Malcolm Balfour.

"I got tired": Malcolm Balfour, in an interview on September 23, 2006.

"The Team Rating System": Iain Calder, in an e-mail sent on January 19, 2007.

"If we can't get an exclusive": Iain Calder, *The Untold Story*, p. 92.

Information for "Ari and Jackie" story: Jim McCandlish, in an e-mail sent on January 30, 2007.

"Money was regarded": John Harris, in an interview on November 17, 2006.

Information and quotes for "The Abominable Snowman" story and "Don't expect to hear": Bob Temmey, in phone interviews given and e-mails sent from September 14, 2007 to October 17, 2007.

The New Soviet Psychic Discoveries, Henry Gris and William Dick: Morag Dick, in an interview on June 13, 2007.

Information for "Behind the Iron Curtain" story: Iain Calder, *The Untold Story*, pp. 117–18.

"It was like": Armando Giacosa, in an interview on September 1, 2007.

"Tears streaming down": "U.S. Admiral United With His Russian 'Love Child,'" *National Enquirer*, April 15, 1975.

Information for "The Search for Utopia": John Harris, in an interview on November 17, 2006, and from a collection of "Search for Utopia" stories: John Harris, unpublished writings, 1990.

Lead sheet: John Harris, "How I Happened to Search for Utopia," unpublished writings, 1990.

Chapter 4. The Brits Are Coming

"Last rites of Fleet Street": www.smh.com/au/nes/business/last-rites-for-fleet-street, June 16, 2005.

"Kill or be killed": Jim McCandlish, in an interview on September 23, 2006.

"Anything Goes": Iain Calder, *The Untold Story*, pp. 10 & 17.

"I was so surprised": Joe West, in an interview on June 11, 2007.

Tabloid package: Jim McCandlish, in an interview on September 23, 2006.

Joe West's job tryout: Joe West, in an interview on June 11, 2007.

"Dummies": Phil Bunton, in an e-mail sent on May 7, 2008.

"When I was editor": Mike Foley, in an e-mail sent on October 19, 2007.

Information for Bing Crosby story: reconstructed from the accounts of several reporters.

"You are only as good": Jim McCandlish, in an interview on September 23, 2006.

"*Enquirer*: Violence Gets the Ax": Malcolm Balfour, *Washington Post*, October 15, 1972.

Information for Uri Geller story and quotes: Malcolm Balfour, in an interview on September 23, 2006, and "Uri Geller Beats Incredible Odds In Spectacular ESP Experiment": Dick Saxty, *National Enquirer*, October 14, 1975, p. 4.

"Sheik Brian Hogan": Iain Calder, *The Untold Story*, pp. 120–21.

Information for "Valley Of Longevity" story: Jim McCandlish, in an interview on September 23, 2006, and in an e-mail sent on October 20, 2007.

Gig Young story: information and quotes derived from interviews with Malcolm Balfour, Jim McCandlish, and David Wright; see also Iain Calder, *The Untold Story*, p. 143.

"I Killed Gig Young": Jay Gourley, *Washington Monthly*, September, 1981.

Blue Anchor Pub: Lee Harrison, in an interview on September 7, 2006.

"From early beginnings": Mike Nevard, in an e-mail sent on September 13, 2007.

Chapter 5. The Rise of Tabloid Valley

"*Star* Promo": World News Corporation, 1973, courtesy of Mike Nevard.

"It was crazy": quote taken from a phone interview with a *Star* reporter who has requested to remain anonymous.

Information for the Elvis Presley story: Iain Calder, *The Untold Story*, pp. 149–52. Also from information provided by Iain Calder in a phone interview on January 10, 2007.

Carol Burnett libel suit: "Enquirer Belted," *Time* magazine, April 6, 1981.

"Pope wanted any bright": Jim McCandlish, in an e-mail sent on May 15, 2008.

First *Weekly World News*: Phil Bunton, in an e-mail sent on May 7, 2008.

"Sometimes at the end of the day": Jack Alexander, in an interview on September 22, 2006.

Eddie Clontz: Craig Pittman, "Tabloid Titan Dies: Elvis In Mourning," *St. Petersburg Times*, January 29, 2004.

Information for "The China Jump" and "Cowboy's Corpse Buried": Jack Alexander, in an interview on September 22, 2006.

Quotes from "Cowboy's Corpse Buried": Jack Alexander, *Weekly World News*, February 9, 1993, pp. 34-35. "My real goal": William R. Amlong, "The High Priest of Lowbrow," *Miami Herald*, January 14, 1973.

Globe and *National Examiner* headlines: S. Elizabeth Bird, *For Enquiring Minds*, extracted from an illustration insert.

Information and quotes for John Belushi story: Larry Haley, in an interview on October 19, 2007, and "I Killed John Belushi": Tony Brenna and Larry Haley, *National Enquirer*, June 29, 1982, pp. 52-53.

"Who was she" and "media explosion": Larry Haley in an interview on October 19, 2007.

"Gary Hart the Elusive Front Runner": E.J. Dionne Jr., *New York Times*, May 3, 1987.

Miami Herald coverage of Gary Hart: Jim McGee, Tom Fiedler, and James Savage, "The Gary Hart Story: How It Happened," *Miami Herald*, May 10, 1987, article accessed at www.unc.edu/pmeyer/Hart/hartarticle.html.

Information for Gary Hart story: Larry Haley, in a phone interview on October 10, 2007. "A Pope Commendation" also was courtesy of Larry Haley.

"Tabloid trash": M. Daly, "The Stench of 'Trash' Comes from John Edwards, not *National Enquirer*," *New York Daily News*, August 10, 2008.

People mission: Norberto Angetti and Alberto Oliva, *Magazines That Make History*, p. 364.

Chapter 6. Post-Pope

"I would like for them to say": Iain Calder, *The Untold Story*, p. 220.

New York Times obituary: appeared on October 3, 1988.

New York Post obituary: Iain Calder, *The Untold Story*, p. 218.

"A good corporate citizen": Michael Bornstein, in an interview on September 23, 2006.

National Enquirer Christmas: information derived from interviews with Jack Carpenter and Michael Bornstein. Also Tracie Cone, "In Training For the Holiday," *Miami Herald*, December 6, 1987.

"Everything died": Jack Carpenter, in a phone interview on August 28, 2007.

"Whoever buys": Michael Allen, "Supermarket Tabloid Shocker! *National Enquirer* Is Up For Sale," *Wall Street Journal*, December 19, 1998.

"A profit of $120 million": Iain Calder, *The Untold Story*, p. 231.

"The *Star* had to be": Dick Kaplan, in a phone interview on August 16, 2007.

"At the reporting level": Steven Edwards, in an interview on March 25, 2007.

Information for *Globe* story: Phil Bunton, in an interview on March 5, 2007.

"Should This Woman Be Named": Margaret Carlson, *Time* magazine, April 29, 1991.

New York Times: Richard Lacayo, "Tarting Up the Gray Lady of 43rd Street," *Time* magazine, May 6, 1991.

"It's Dallas": Walter Goodman, "For TV, It's a Little Bit of Everything," *New York Times*, December 5, 1991.

"Our hope is": "*Globe* Prints Name, Photo of Alleged Rape Victim," *Palm Beach Post*, April 16, 1991.

"This isn't Martians": "Behind the *Star*'s Headlines," *Time* magazine, February 3, 1992.

"Back to the business": Dick Kaplan, in a phone interview on August 16, 2007.

Information for Gennifer Flowers story: Steven Edwards, in an interview on March 25, 2007.

"Bill Clinton, Gennifer Flowers and Me": Steven Edwards, *Saturday Midnight*, May 1998.

"The *Star* was the first": Steven Edwards, in an interview on March 25, 2007.

"Feed the Press": Paula Span and Laurie Goodstein, "The Bright & Slimy *Star*; Checking Out the Tabloid That Ran With the Clinton Story," *Washington Post*, January 28, 1992.

"Endless Questions": Amy E. Schwartz, *Washington Post*, January 29, 1992.

"And the *Enquirer*'s Kind": Andrea Sachs, "Mud and the Mainstream," *Columbia Journalism Review*, May/June, 1995, p. 1.

"All drinking from the same trough": Steven LeGrice, in an interview on August 16, 2007.

Information for O. J. Simpson story: David Perel, in an interview on June 12, 2007; also Iain Calder, *The Untold Story*, p. 274. Finally, "How *Enquirer* Scooped the World On O. J.": *National Enquirer*, August 24, 2004.

"The *Enquirer*: Required Reading in Simpson Case": David Margolick, *New York Times*, October 24, 1994.

"Jammed a big story": Dick Kaplan, in an interview on October 8, 2007.

"O. J. was the biggest tabloid story": Phil Bunton, in an interview on March 5, 2007.

Information and quotes for "The Bruno Magli Shoes" story: Larry Haley, in an interview on June 20, 2007.

"It was like an onion": Steven LeGrice, in an interview on August 16, 2007.

"Money in the bank": Phil Bunton, in an interview on March 5, 2007.

"The Tabloid Decade": David Kamp, *Vanity Fair*, February, 1999.

Chapter 7. The Influence of Tabloid Valley

"If Elvis was dead": Steven LeGrice, in an interview on August 16, 2007.

"As tabloids": Phil Bunton, in an interview on March 5, 2007.

Reference to *Time* magazine "The Man Who": Richard L. Berke, "Call-Girl Story Cost President a Key Strategist," *New York Times*, August 30, 1997.

"There was a good": Richard Goodling quoted in Richard Zoglin's, "Inquiring Minds Want To Know: Is This Story True," *Time* magazine, September 9, 1996.

"We knew they": Phil Bunton, in an interview on March 29, 2007.

"Sadistic vitriol of yellow journalism": Maureen Dowd, "Sadistic Yellow Vitriol," *New York Times*, September 1, 1996.

"As happened so often": Richard Zoglin, "Inquiring Minds Want To Know: Is This Story True," *Time* magazine, September 9, 1996.

Information for "A Back Story": Phil Bunton, in an e-mail sent on May 23, 2007.

"What was so notable": Jodie Morse, "His Just Reward," *Time* magazine, July 20, 1998.

"The *Enquirer*'s reward": Christian Berthelsen, "Tabloid Offers Reward and Gets Small Thanks," *New York Times*, July 6, 1998.

"*Time*'s 25 Most Influential Americans": *Time* magazine, April 21, 1997.

"Going back before": Roy Peter Clark, in an interview on August 29, 2006.

The "DNA" of the *National Enquirer*": David Perel, in an interview on June 12, 2007.

"Every Single network": Steve Coz in "*Time*'s 25 Most Influential Americans," *Time* magazine, April 21, 1997.

"Rock-solid tabloid": Tony Frost in *US* magazine, cited in Bill Sloan's, *I Watched A Wild Hog Eat My Baby*, p. 198.

"When Tabloids Cross the Line": Steve Coz, *New York Times*, May 29, 1997.

"Death Photos For Sale: $250,000": www.usatoday.com/news/diana28.htm, updated 07/08/99.

"Blood money": Phil Bunton, in an interview on April 25, 2007.

"We will not bid": David Perel in "The World Mourns A Once-Shy Woman Who Outshined Royalty, 'The People's Princess,'" *Palm Beach Post*, September 1, 1997.

Information for Princess Grace story: Joanna Elm, in an interview on June 23, 2007.

"We told": Steve Coz in Margaret Carlson's, "Blood On Their Hands," *Time* magazine, September 8, 1997.

"Whether I'm paranoid": Phil Bunton, in an e-mail sent on April 25, 2007.

National Enquirer specials and the Hurricane Planning Center: Mike Nevard, in an interview on June 9, 2007.

"No Bad Dogs": Emily Hamer-West, in an interview on September 30, 2007.

Rafe Klinger's headline: Bill Sloan, *I Watched A Wild Hog Eat My Baby*, p. 173.

"Elvis Is Alive": Joe West's story is reproduced from an e-mail sent on April 9, 2007.

"TOH": John Harris, in an e-mail sent on April 12, 2007.

"TOH" hurricane dog story and quotes: Al Fayette, in an interview on September 3, 2007.

"*National Examiner* Inter-Office Memo": distributed September 3, 1993.

"Blurred the boundaries": Janny Scott, "A Media Race Enters Waters Still Uncharted," *New York Times*, February 1, 1998.

"Lamented that most": Steve Coz in "Publishers, Tabloids Dangle Millions For Lewinsky Tell-All," *Palm Beach Post*, September 3, 1998.

"My sense": John Waters in David Kamp's, "The Tabloid Decade," *Vanity Fair*, February 1999.

Average sales figures: Iain Calder, *The Untold Story*, p. 295.

Chapter 8. The Tabloid Valley Enters the New Millennium

"It's going to be open warfare": Phil Bunton, in an interview on March 5, 2005.

"I think it will": "Enquirer Owner Buys *Globe* To Corner Market," *Palm Beach Post*, November 3, 1999.

"I want to build": Paul Owers, "*Enquirer* To Continue Affairs in P. B. County," *Palm Beach Post*, July 9, 1999.

"Acquisition binge": Stephanie Smith and Paul Owers, "American Media Aims To Be Major Force," *Palm Beach Post*, February 17, 2000.

"The Focus has changed" and "entertainment junkies": David Perel, in an interview on June 12, 2007.

"Saucy, bold tabloid": Stephanie Smith, "*National Enquirer* Gets New Look," *Palm Beach Post*, October 2, 1999.

Information for Tammy Faye Bakker story: Jim McCandlish, in an interview on July 19, 2007.

"Dying Bible Queen": Jim McCandlish and Pat Gregor, "Tammy Faye's Farewell Party," *Globe*, June 4, 2007.

"OMIGOD" covers: Bonnie Fuller in "Diva Of Celebrity Journalism," CBS News, November 24, 2004.

"A lot of the traditional": Deborah Solomon, "Too Much Isn't Enough," *New York Times*, March 26, 2006.

"From Liz to Britney": Larry Haley, in an e-mail sent on June 22, 2007.

"But we went up against" and "Was the severance": "Clarence Page On Jesse Jackson," *Columbia Journalism Review*, January 1, 2002.

"Meeting his obligations": Michael Hanrahan and Patricia Sharp, "Jesse Jackson's Love Child," *National Enquirer*, January 30, 2001, p. 20.

Information for Hugh Rodham story: David Wright, in a phone interview on August 16, 2007.

"Slam dunk story": Michael Isikoff, "*National Enquirer* Gets Scoop on Presidential Pardons," Reliable Sources, CNN, aired February 24, 2001.

Information and quotes for Afghanistan story: Alan Butterfield, in a phone interview on June 28, 2007, and "Bin Laden Terrorist Tells All," *National Enquirer*, October 9, 2001.

"Don't worry, no problem": Saeed to Alan Butterfield, obtained from a phone interview with Butterfield on June 28, 2007.

September 11 and the tabloids: S. Elizabeth Bird, "Taking It Personally," *Journalism After September 11*, p. 148.

Information and quotes for Anthrax story: "Bio-Terroism: the Florida Anthrax Attack on *Enquirer* Headquarters": *National Enquirer*, October 2, 2001.

Recollections of Anthrax experience: taken over the course of many interviews with AMI staff.

"He had the eye," Bob Stevens: Tom Wilbur, in a phone interview on May 30, 2007.

"Tab Lloyd": Rick Harlowe, in an e-mail sent on June 2, 2007.

"I never, never dreamed": Eliot Kleinberg, *Palm Beach Post*, August 27, 2002.

"A Bigger Story" and "We cover stories": David Wright, in a phone interview on June 12, 2007.

"The company wants": "*Enquirer* to Jettison New York for Boca," *Palm Beach Post*, April 6, 2006.

"They were heavily leveraged": Martin Walker in Jeff Ostrowski's, "AMI Bleeds $160 Million," *Palm Beach Post*, March 30, 2007.

Chapter 9. The Future of Tabloid Valley

Weekly World News Wake: Rick Harlow, in an e-mail circulated on July 25, 2007.

"We're fun," Billy Burt: S. Elizabeth Bird, *For Enquiring Minds*, p. 91.

"Wit and raconteur": Family-placed funeral notice, *Palm Beach Post*, March 21, 2007.

"He was one of the most colorful": Ron Hayes, "Billy Burt, Colorful *National Enquirer* Reporter," *Palm Beach Post*, March 20, 2007.

"I'm working for this crazy outfit": Jim McCandlish, in an e-mail sent on February 27, 2008.

Information for *Star* as a glossy magazine: Steven LeGrice, in an e-mail sent on June 6, 2008.

Information and quotes for Mariah Carey story: Dorothy Cascerceri, in a phone interview on February 20, 2008, and "Secret of Hot New Body": Dorothy Cascerceri, *National Enquirer*, October 8, 2007, p. 37.

Opinions about the future of the tabloids are taken from responses to my query, "Tabloids, in one form or another, have existed for several hundred years. How will these publications survive in the era of cable television and the Internet, where scandal and celebrity news are available 24 hours a day?"

Bibliography

Bernard, George. *Inside the National Enquirer: Confessions of an Undercover Reporter.* Port Washington, N.Y.: Ashley Books, 1977.

Bessie, Simon Michael. *Jazz Journalism: The Story of the Tabloid Newspapers.* New York: E.P. Dutton & Co., 1938.

Bird, S. Elizabeth. *For Enquiring Minds: A Cultural Study of Supermarket Tabloids.* Knoxville: University of Tennessee Press, 1992.

Bleyer, Willard Grosvenor. *Main Currents in the History of American Journalism.* New York: Houghton Mifflin, 1927.

Calder, Iain. *The Untold Story: My 20 Years Running the National Enquirer.* New York: Miramax Books/Hyperion, 2004.

Cuozzo, Steven. *It's Alive: How America's Oldest Newspaper Cheated Death and Why It Matters.* New York: Times Books, 1996.

Ehrlich, Matthew C. *The Journalism of Outrageousness: Tabloid Television News vs. Investigative News.* Columbia, S.C.: Association for Education in Journalism and Mass Communication, 1996.

Glynn, Kevin. *Tabloid Culture.* Durham, N.C.: Duke University Press, 2000.

Gris, Henry, and William Dick. *The New Soviet Psychic Discoveries.* New York: Warner Books, 1978.

Horrie, Chris. *Tabloid Nation: The Birth of the Daily Mirror to the Death of the Tabloid.* London: Andre Deutsch, Ltd., 2003.

Keeps, David, Charles Melcher, and Valerie Virga. *The National Enquirer: Thirty Years of Unforgettable Images.* New York: Miramax Books/Hyperion, 2001.

Mallen, Frank. *Sauce for the Gander*. White Plains, N.Y.: Baldwin Books, 1954.

Schudson, Michael. *Discovering the News: A Social History of American Newspapers*. New York: Basic Books, 1978.

Sloan, Bill. *I Watched a Wild Hog Eat My Baby!* Amherst, N.Y.: Prometheus Books, 2001.

Taylor, S.J. *Shock! Horror! The Tabloids in Action*. New York: Bantam Press, 1991.

Vitek, Jack. *The Godfather of Tabloid: Generoso Pope Jr. and the National Enquirer*. Lexington: University Press of Kentucky, 2008.

Walls, Jeannette. *Dish*. New York: Harper Collins, 2000.

Waters, John. *Crackpot!* New York: Vintage Books, 1987.

Index

EXCLUSIVE...

Paula E. Morton left the native plant nursery and flock of sheep she tended on her Pennsylvania farm to live in beautiful St. Augustine, Florida. A freelance writer, she ventures beyond the treasures of this environment to explore the history and culture of the supermarket tabloids.